# FRIENDS
# HELPERS
# LOVERS

**For Chris, Steve, DD and Ali**

With our love, gratitude
and some words of wisdom:

*There is one thing that makes a husband great*
*– the respect of his wife.*

*There is one thing that makes a wife great*
*– the love of her husband.*

*There are two things that make children great*
*– their parents!*

# FRIENDS
# HELPERS
# LOVERS

## the early years of marriage

## IAN & RUTH COFFEY

INTER-VARSITY PRESS

INTER-VARSITY PRESS
*38 De Montfort Street, Leicester LE1 7GP, England*

*First published 1996*

**British Library Cataloguing in Publication Data**
A catalogue record for this book is available from the British
Library.

ISBN 0–85111–174–2


Set in Franklin Gothic
Typeset in Great Britain by Avocet Typeset, Brill,
Aylesbury, Bucks
Printed in Great Britain by Cox and Wyman Ltd,
Reading, Berks

*Inter-Varsity Press is the book-publishing division of the
Universities and Colleges Christian Fellowship (formerly the
Inter-Varsity Fellowship), a student movement linking Christian
Unions in universities and colleges throughout the United
Kingdom and the Republic of Ireland, and a member movement
of the International Fellowship of Evangelical Students. For
information about local and national activities write to UCCF,
38 De Montfort Street, Leicester LE1 7GP*

# CONTENTS

# CONTENTS

# PREFACE

It is not an easy thing to write a book.

It is not an easy thing to write a book with someone else.

It is not an easy thing to write a book with your marriage partner.

It is not an easy thing to write a book about marriage with your marriage partner.

As you may have guessed, this has not been an easy book to write!

Now the excuses are out of the way, we can get on with the business of telling you what's in store over the next few chapters.

There's a standard best man's wedding gag that goes: *'I can remember when I got married. And where I got married. What I just can't remember is, why?'*

This book is about what he'd forgotten.

We have written it with a particular audience in mind. If you are planning to marry or are in your first few years of married life, then this book is for you. Mind you, we can imagine all sorts of other people taking a sneaky glance, and if you are one of those – you are welcome too.

We have attempted to keep several rules under our noses. One has been to write as honestly as we can. We are still wearing our 'L' plates so far as marriage and family life goes, and like most people we have had our fair share of bumps and scrapes. We have tried hard to be honest in what we have written in the belief that playing 'let's pretend' is a game for children, not grown-ups.

Another thing we have done is to write personally. You may find that a little difficult at times. For instance, your experience or personalities may be vastly different from ours. But we hope you will hear something that is repeated several times in the book: every marriage is unique. The principles remain the same – but the way of working them out will vary in each relationship.

To give an example, some time back we received a letter from a couple who had read something we had written about marriage. They pointed out (very politely!) that we had assumed that the 'traditional' roles for men and women were the only way for a successful marriage to operate. They went on to explain how they had decided early on in married life to reverse roles. They made a conscious choice for the wife to be the main breadwinner, and her partner became a househusband. Their letter detailed how this had brought great fulfilment to them as individuals and also to their children.

As we said when we replied, God leads us all in different ways, and it was good to read of their positive experience. They had found something that worked for them and were happy to share their discovery with others.

This book is rather like the story of the centipede and the owl. The centipede was struggling with aching legs (and he had rather a lot of them too), so he turned to the wisest creature for advice, the owl. 'It's simple,' the owl told him, 'you need to stop walking and start flying. Your legs will feel better in no time.' The centipede thought for a moment. 'Sounds good,' he responded. 'Just one problem though. How can I learn to fly?' 'Listen,' the owl replied, 'I just give you the principles – you have to work out the details yourself!'

Every relationship is different, and we hope that the principles shared in these pages will enable you to work together on the details that fit your own circumstances. That means you might not always agree with our conclusions, but if what we have written helps you to 'think Christianly' about the principles of marriage, we will be more than satisfied.

Another rule we have tried to stick to is to be as practical as we can be. You will find we use examples of real-life people – although, for obvious reasons, we have changed their names. Practical examples of how various couples have faced the joys and pressures of married life are, we believe, one of the ways we learn the skills of relationship-building. We apologize if at times we appear to state the obvious. Our experience suggests that many people struggle to understand the basics about a Christian view of marriage because we have assumed too much.

We hope that you find *Friends, Helpers, Lovers* helpful in building your marriage. You will notice we have included a study guide on pages 185–190. If you are reading this alone, or as a couple, we hope it will help to earth the material in each chapter. If you are reading the book as part of a marriage preparation group, then the questions may form a basis for discussion. Either way, the questions are there to encourage you to get talking!

God never intended marriage to be a duet. It's a trio. And twenty-something years on, we recognize that the best tunes happen when there are three sets of hands – not two – on the keys.

*Ian and Ruth Coffey*
*Plymouth, England*
*December 1995*

# ACKNOWLEDGMENTS

Our thanks go to a group of people who have helped in the preparation of this book:

Sylvia Backaller and Tim Searle provided some useful background research and information. Yvonne Morris read the manuscript and offered a number of perceptive comments.

Karen Tunstall balanced the many other responsibilities in her busy life to patiently work and re-work the manuscript into a readable form.

The Barling and Giles families loaned us 'Cuilan' which gave us peace and space to think and write.

And our four sons (to whom this book is dedicated) have given us ... plenty to think about!

Stephanie Heald at IVP has been as professional and supportive an editor as we could hope for.

There are also many married couples – and single friends as well – who have shared insights which have shaped our attitudes to marriage and family.

Some friends have said little – but the quality of their relationships has said it all.

We also thank God for parents who gave us the foundation of a good homelife, a great deal of love and the investment of their prayers.

# CHAPTER ONE

# HAPPILY
## EVER AFTER?

The bride wore white; the bridegroom, a new suit. Family and friends said what a lovely couple they made. She looked so young. But on this day of days she looked so beautiful that she glowed. He looked shy and vulnerable, displaying a positive dislike both of his new suit and of the photographer, who kept insisting, 'Look this way – and look happy!' But when he stole a glance at her, and forgot the crowd with their clicking cameras, you could see a warmth come over him. They exchanged their smiles and knowing glances as only a couple in love can do. He tried not to keep looking at his watch as the reception dragged by. She tried not to show her embarrassment as dad rambled on about not losing a daughter but gaining a son. And mum got quite emotional.

At last, they were off. A hasty get-away in his car, which friends had seen fit to decorate with crazy-foam slogans, tin cans and a few balloons. As they rattled down the street, their friends and relatives shouting good wishes, they could hardly believe it. The day was over almost before it had started.

For two people a whole new life had begun. With confetti down their necks, a rented flat with secondhand furniture, a brand new double bed (interior-sprung, posture mattress), a handful of hopes, and eyes only for each other, they grasped, with nervous hands, one of the greatest gifts God has ever given – marriage.

But where will it all end? The fairy tales tell us that the handsome prince marries the beautiful princess and they both live happily ever after. We would all like our stories to end that way, but, sadly, in real life, it does not always happen. In the West, around a third of marriages end in divorce; in some countries the figure is higher. Second and even third marriages go wrong at a high rate. Marriage is in crisis because people are in crisis. We need urgently to get back to the Maker and his instructions.

Marriage needs to be worked at. That is such an important statement that we will repeat it. Marriage needs to be worked at. If you like woven texts on walls, try that, in bright red letters a metre high. Marriage needs to be worked at! Hang a copy in your living-room, over your bed, at the sink, and on the front door. *Marriage needs to be worked at!*

You may both be deeply committed Christians with a confidence that God has led you to each other. Please do not think that problems and pressures in marriage happen only to other couples. The fact that God has brought you together makes you a particular target. *Your* marriage needs to be worked at.

## 'Those magnificent men in their flying machines'

Have you ever heard of someone trying to fly a plane without bothering to take lessons? Well, if so, that was probably the only time you heard of him or her! Before letting anyone loose at the controls of an aircraft there are hours of instruction, in the classroom as well as the cockpit. Then there is an examination to discover if the prospective pilot understood the lessons. A friend of ours who is a commercial airline pilot with many flying hours behind him recently underwent a training course for 747s, jumbo jets. In spite of years of experience in different parts of the world, no-one was prepared to let him loose on the controls until he had met the required standard, and that took a lot of hard work. But the next time you fasten yourself into an aircraft seat, you will feel a lot safer in the knowledge that the pilot has had to prove himself or herself before taking on the responsibility for hundreds of lives. The same rules apply in other areas of life: driving a car, teaching a pre-school kindergarten, performing delicate eye surgery or directing rush-hour traffic. We accept that for complicated jobs, human beings need training.

The potential disaster of a wrecked marriage can be as great, if not greater, than any car accident. Lives are delicate and need to be handled with care. Behind today's well-worn euphemism, 'a broken home', there lies a lot of truth. Broken homes mean broken marriages, broken promises, broken lives, broken hearts – broken people.

How is it that although we will not let anyone get behind the wheel of a car or on to the flight deck of an aircraft without proper instruction, we allow people to stumble into marriage with no more than a shout of 'Good luck!', a few nudge-nudge comments and a food processor? When marriages go wrong, people get hurt. And sometimes the wounds inflicted never heal.

We are writing this book with the conviction that there are no experts in marriage, only learners. We need to learn from one another – but, most important of all, we need to learn from God.

## God created marriage

God invented marriage, and, as always, he created something good. It is one of his choicest gifts to men and women, with the potential for being well used or abused. In Genesis God reveals to us how and why marriage came into being. 'The LORD God said, "It is not good for the man to be alone. I will make a helper suitable for him"' (Gn. 2:18). God saw that human loneliness was not a good thing. And God in creation was concerned with creating only good things. He moved in his creative power to fulfil the man's deep need of companionship. God brought the animals and birds before Adam for them to be named, but none of them fitted his need for a mate. The Bible continues:

> So the LORD God caused the man to fall into a deep sleep; and while he was sleeping, he took one of the man's ribs and closed up the place with flesh. Then the LORD God made a woman from the rib he had taken out of the man, and he brought her to the man.
>
> The man said,
>
> > 'This is now bone of my bones
> >    and flesh of my flesh;
> > she shall be called "woman",
> >    for she was taken out of man.'

Adam found God's design delightful. Woman was part of him and yet different from him. They fitted perfectly – a reflection of the Creator in whose image they were made.

Then comes a vitally important statement that is loaded with truth about marriage: 'For this reason a man will leave his father and mother and be united to his wife, and they will become one flesh. The man and his wife were both naked, and they felt no shame' (Gn. 2:24–25). Notice the first three words: 'For *this* reason'. In the light of all that has been said about Adam's need of companionship, God's creation of woman and Adam's delight at her perfection – for this reason marriage has been ordained as a gift from God.

Charles Swindoll, the author and Christian leader, has written helpfully on these two verses as providing four foundational guidelines for a meaningful marriage.

- *Severance:* 'a man will leave his father and mother'
- *Permanence:* 'and be united to his wife'
- *Unity:* 'and they will become one flesh'

▶ *Intimacy:* 'and the man and his wife were both naked, and they felt no shame'

Swindoll comments: 'Without wanting to oversimplify marital conflicts and complications, I can say that in most every difficulty I have dealt with, one or more of these guidelines were either ignored or violated. They are the basis to domestic harmony.'[1]

God created marriage and God makes marriages. It is not luck that we need, but God's help in understanding how two complex, sinful human beings can live together in love and harmony. That is why, in these chapters, we want to take a practical look at the Maker's instructions on marriage.

## All you need is love

It is just possible that you feel that the heavy emphasis on working at marriage does not apply to you. Other people have their marital ups and downs, but never you. We are not denying the possibility that you are blissfully happy, nor are we wanting anyone to feel deprived if there are no pressing problems at the moment. We simply urge you to recognize that even the most mature and balanced Christians find that their marriages come under pressure at different times. Forewarned should mean forearmed. Let us share with you some actual instances of Christian marriages under pressure.

Mark and Jackie, on the surface, appeared to be a happily married couple. They were both active in their local church and were progressing well in their respective careers. But, after several years of marriage, they had never achieved full sexual intercourse. Jackie had deep fears rooted in childhood, when she had been sexually abused. This meant that she was afraid of an intimate physical relationship. To the casual observer she appeared to be a happy, extrovert woman, but in actual fact this was a mask intended to hide a very hurt and insecure person underneath.

At first Mark, although disappointed, had been patient and understanding. He hoped that with time Jackie would relax sufficiently to allow full intercourse to take place. But the situation grew worse. Weeks became months and, despite Mark's repeated suggestions that they should consult their doctor, Jackie refused. Eventually, sex became a taboo subject between them. Mark became sullen and withdrawn. Jackie, who was racked with guilt, convinced herself that if she ignored the problem it would sort itself out one day.

They kept up appearances to family and friends, but behind closed doors they became two strangers. After some years the situation deteriorated to such an extent that Mark announced he was leaving. Whether or not there was someone else, Jackie could not tell, but the shock of his announcement brought her to earth with a bump. Within a few days, Jackie had shared her devastating news with a close Christian friend. Help and professional advice were offered and Jackie gratefully accepted. She even agreed to visit the doctor, admitting that this should have taken place at the very start. At last the problem was out in the open and Jackie felt she could face it.

But something had happened to Mark. Frustration had gnawed away at him. He had no doubt that once he had loved Jackie. But over the months he had found his suppressed anger turning to spite. Spiritually he felt he had died on the inside. He kept up attendances at church and appearances among friends, but the real Mark had become a cynical agnostic. Jackie was willing, at long last, to do something; Mark had lost the desire even to try. They had grown up as teenagers in the swinging sixties when sexual 'liberation' was so commonplace it became boring. You might have thought that frankness about sexuality would have made it easier for Mark and Jackie to share their problem. But quite the opposite was the case. Surrounded by those who are allegedly goldmedallists in sex, who likes to admit that the zip on their tracksuit is stuck?

Sadly, the offer of help came too late for Mark and Jackie. Their marriage ended in annulment with a court ruling that it had never been consummated. Two Christians, plus their immediate families, were left devastated. What a terribly expensive way to learn that ignoring a problem never solves it!

For Richard and Sue, their problem was so basic it has become a joke. They say human beings always laugh at things they fear. That is why we have jokes about death, dentists, sex and mothers-in-law.

But for Richard and Sue, mother-in-law gave them nothing to laugh about. Richard was an only child and, much to his mother's relief, decided to buy a home near to his parents when he married. He and Sue moved to an adjoining street and, while they were both out at work, the nearness of Sue's in-laws posed no real problems. After a few years, Sue became pregnant with their first child and it was around this time that Richard's mum began her unscheduled visits. During the end of her pregnancy and the first few months of adjusting to their new baby, Sue found her mother-in-law a great help. She knew that she could never have coped with their new arrival without her support, which only increased her sense of guilt when she found herself beginning to resent her mother-in-law's intrusions.

Sue's own mother lived far away and was unable to provide such regular help. This produced an element of rivalry between the parents, and Sue found herself becoming defensive at some of the remarks Richard's mother made concerning the lack of visits the new grandson was getting from the 'other side of the family'.

Richard's mother would arrive at any time of the day or night and never used the front door. She would open the kitchen door and, with a cry of 'It's me!' she would be in. She would interrupt meals, baby's bedtime, and television program- mes. On one occasion, Richard and Sue were making love in the early evening when the mother's voice was heard in the kitchen, causing a frantic search for clothes! They laugh- ed about it afterwards, but inwardly Sue found her anger building up to such an extent that she could no longer keep it to herself. Sue shared it with their pastor and his wife who urged her to talk it through with Richard. But he could not see the problem, and what started out as a level-headed conversation ended in a blazing row, with Sue in floods of tears and Richard claiming she was ungrateful in spurning his mother's help.

There are two sides to every story. But for Sue, the situation was becoming increasingly desperate. She was becoming deeply depressed and found herself, at times, beginning to resent their lovely baby boy, who had taken her freedom away and created a situation where her life was no longer her own and their home seemed a public park.

As matters reached boiling-point, Richard and Sue went back to their minister desperate for help. The advice they received was clear and helpful, and the prayer and support over the next few months saw them through the crisis which threatened to wreck their marriage. Step one was an honest but painful conversation between Richard and his mother in which he laid out some guidelines about her visiting their home.

Relations were cool for some time between Sue and her mother-in-law. But Sue made a point of including her in various family events and worked hard at making her feel loved and appreciated. Eventually, Richard and Sue moved to a larger house but, with their relationship more secure than it had ever been, they made the conscious choice to live several miles away from the in-laws.

Paul and Joanne were great friends of Tony and Sally. They

attended the same church and were constantly in and out of each other's homes. Paul was involved in youth leadership and Joanne had been one of his small team of helpers. But now, with three small children, they both felt that her priorities lay at home while the children were young. Paul desperately needed help, so he asked Sally to join him. Tony and Sally had two children who were a few years older than his three. Tony was willing to commit himself to staying in one evening each week to allow Sally the freedom to work with the young people. They both felt this was a useful piece of Christian service, and Tony was in full agreement with his wife's involvement.

Paul and Sally saw a lot of each other. In addition to the young people's meetings, they met for planning meetings and frequently called each other on the telephone to discuss various problems in the group. Without consciously noticing, they had become strongly attached to each other. Paul and Joanne were happily married with a strong relationship. But Tony and Sally had been experiencing tensions for some time. Tony had a demanding job which caused him to work long hours and sometimes to be away on business trips. Sally felt, at times, neglected and a runner-up to the company in Tony's list of priorities. Physically their relationship had been 'off the boil' for a few months, with Tony feeling too tired and Sally too resentful.

Paul, on the other hand, paid a good deal of attention to Sally, often commenting on how attractive she looked or how much he liked her in a particular outfit. He made these comments with the best will in the world, because he saw that at times she looked down and tired. Sally responded to the compliments with warmth, again not with wrong motives, but because she felt pleased to be noticed.

Not many people wake up in the morning and consciously think, 'Today I am going to commit adultery; I intend to be unfaithful to my partner.' Adultery is something you drift into. Of course it takes a deliberate act. But long before the act comes the thought. And often, long before the thought, come the circumstances that accelerate temptation's powerful pull. In the pages of the Bible we discover we are not the first to suffer like this. One example is the story of Joseph who, when confronted with the persistence of a woman who wanted a sexual relationship with him, found the best way to deal with it was to run – and as fast as he could (Gn. 39:12). There are times when we find ourselves drifting into dangerous situations and need to turn around and run from them.

Paul and Sally had some good friends who were helping them in their young people's work. These friends had noticed how involved the relationship had become, and loved them enough to do something about it. Instead of sitting back and gossiping, the husband approached Paul and told him of his concern. Paul (who by this time was falling head over heels for Sally) dismissed the suggestion as ridiculous. The friends took the matter to the elders in their church fellowship, who immediately arranged to see Paul and Sally and their partners, Tony and Joanne.

It was a painful time. Thankfully, Paul and Sally were strong enough in their Christian commitment to have remained faithful to their partners. But emotionally they had become bound up with one another, to such an extent that it took a long time for them to get sorted out. Paul and Joanne left the church, under the advice of their leaders, and moved to a new area. Tony and Sally had to make changes in their own relationship, particularly Tony, who began to deal with the deficiencies in his attitude towards his work and family life. A major moral and spiritual crisis was avoided in this local church – a crisis which would have affected many people, some of them young and vulnerable. But there was (and still is) a lot of hurt and brokenness that needs healing.

Peter and Barbara started out on married life full of good intentions. They had high standards for a home, a marriage and a family. They were totally devoted to each other – and that was a large part of the problem.

Peter had a job that involved a considerable amount of travelling, leaving him only the weekends to concentrate on the decorating and alterations to their new home. Barbara worked too, and, as they spent so many hours apart during the week, they enjoyed having the weekends on their own. As a result, they made few friends. They had moved from their home town, mainly because they could not afford to live there. But in their new community, despite having a number of lively Christian churches nearby, they did not really settle down. Within a short time Barbara became pregnant and left work. They were by now attending a local church, but usually just put in a quick appearance at Sunday morning worship and then went home to the decorating. When their baby arrived, it was weeks before they appeared at church. Things were in a vicious circle. Peter and Barbara felt that no-one really cared, and the church gained the impression that this self-sufficient couple wanted to keep people at arm's length and would resent outside interference.

With their high standards for family life, Peter and Barbara took the decision that they would not go to church unless they could go as a family. This left them as 'oncers', with Sunday mornings being the only time they could take the baby with them. But babies get coughs and colds, and often find it difficult to settle in a crèche, and before long church attendance was a rare event for Peter and Barbara.

Rootless and spiritually dried out, they found themselves beginning to drift in their relationship with God. They had often been vocal in their criticism of friends who appeared to be over-involved in Christian activities, and were determined to be much more balanced in their own use of time. But in their desire to build a strong marriage and a nice home, they had overreached themselves and cut themselves off from the Christian fellowship they so badly needed.

Peter and Barbara have never really sorted things out. The children (they now have two) are growing up fast, and although the couple now have more time to get involved, their will-power has gone. Their lifestyle has become very inward-looking. A piece of paper somewhere says that they belong to such and such a church, but in practical terms of Christian fellowship and service they may just as well be living on an iceberg in the mid-Atlantic. Their sad story is repeated many times over. A couple with so much to give have buried themselves away. Rather like the man in the parable that Jesus told, instead of using what they have been given, they have selfishly dug a hole and buried their gift in the ground, opting for the security of selfishness rather than the risks of faith.

David and Rachel were the sort of couple that Peter and Barbara held up as bad examples. They had been married a year, and if you asked either of them if they were happy they would automatically answer 'Of course!' without even stopping to think about the question. But they were not happy. There were nagging tensions beneath the surface of a seemingly normal Christian marriage.

They had grown up in a large church where things were always happening. They were both involved in leading the young people's group, and David and Rachel had agreed that this should continue after their wedding.

The problem centred on the fact that they never had time alone. One Sunday morning a visiting minister had touched on tensions in marriage during his sermon and they both asked to see him at the close of the service. He had spoken as if he knew their home life intimately. It was as though he had experienced the same lack of something they both found hard to express. As they shared together, the minister began asking questions about their marriage and their attitudes to one another. Then he asked a telling question, 'How much time do the two of you spend on your own?'

David and Rachel looked at each other with puzzlement.

'When was the last time you went out together for a meal, or spent the evening by yourselves?' the minister enquired.

They could not remember. Later, as they reflected and checked back on the diary, they discovered, to their horror, that in a year of marriage they had shared no more than two or three evenings alone.

David and Rachel worked in separate places, rushed home for a quick meal, and then were caught up with activities at the church, Bible studies and counselling sessions with young people at home. They would be on the go until late at night, then up early for work the next day. David and Rachel hardly had time to breathe, let alone make love, talk, laugh, or watch a film on TV. Of course, they did pray together. But it is possible to pray together and still hit problems in your marriage, especially if there is no space to be normal human beings. It takes time to develop a relationship, and in our helter-skelter world of constant activity, Christians, above all people, should demonstrate the peace of a God-ordered life.

The church that David and Rachel had grown up in had not helped much. To look at them you would have thought Jesus said, 'I have come that you might have meetings – and have them abundantly!' No-one in the leadership had spotted the danger of a young couple having no time to themselves. The philosophy of this particular church was that 'we are saved to serve', which has much to commend it. But for this young couple, a bit of 'we are born for balance' was what they needed to hear.

It did not take long for David and Rachel to get back on course. They had to make some drastic changes in their diary, and that included one night a week when the phone was off the hook and the doorbell went unanswered. They had to learn to communicate with each other in a deeper way than before. Perhaps the biggest lesson David and Rachel learned was to plan life a little more, rather than letting events dictate what should happen. The art of creating space is a much-neglected area of teaching for Christian couples. David and Rachel learned the lesson early enough to make the changes that were needed.

Andy and Linda were young Christians when they first met. They attended a small church when they were courting, and after their wedding they began to attend a much larger fellowship near to their new home.

Andy was quiet and withdrawn by temperament, whereas Linda was a warm, outgoing person who quickly made friends. She soon became actively involved in the new church and eagerly took on the task of helping to run a young wives' group. Andy had a job that involved shift work, and this meant that several Sundays would pass before they were able to go to church together. Coupled with the problems of work, Andy found conversation hard-going with people he did not know well and, although Linda settled into their new spiritual home, he felt a complete outsider.

After two years their first child was born, and a couple of years later their second baby arrived. During this time Linda kept up her diligent commitment to the church, getting involved fully in the life of the fellowship. Even the arrival of two babies and the many adjustments that they bring to home life did not affect Linda's willingness to be heavily involved in Christian activities. She was a popular person, not only to the vicar and his wife who counted her as one of their key workers, but also in the young wives' group which she led with great enthusiasm. Linda started to help with the visitation ministry of the church, often taking flowers to elderly people or calling with a welcome card when a new family moved into the parish.

Andy progressed in his job, and was in many ways a good husband and father. He felt miles behind Linda in his Christian life and, although he attended church services as often as he could, felt all the while that the closer his wife got to God, the further he was drifting away.

Linda was not at all satisfied with this state of affairs. After a series of sermons entitled 'The Christian Family', she tackled Andy on his total lack of spiritual leadership in the home. There followed several disastrous weeks when they attempted to have family prayers at the breakfast table. Picture the scene: Andy, resentful and unsure of himself, trying to read a far-from-easy passage from the Old Testament about some bloodthirsty battle; Gavin, their eldest, fidgeting because he wanted to go to the toilet; Elizabeth, the baby, tipping the milk-jug over the tablecloth, and Linda's frustration rising to screaming pitch. Family prayers were abandoned after the unsuccessful experimentation period. Andy felt even more of a failure, and Linda, unwisely, began to make it an open secret within the church that her marriage was in trouble.

The vicar called to see Linda one day and she began to talk about the tensions in her relationship with Andy, which were now affecting all aspects of their family life. 'The problem', Linda confided in the vicar, 'is that my husband is just not interested in spiritual things. Perhaps I married the wrong man.'

Fortunately for them both, the vicar and his wife were a perceptive couple who had seen for some months the build-up of tension between Linda and Andy. Gently the vicar began to share with Linda how her marriage looked from the outside. 'I don't think for one moment you married the wrong man. I believe part of the problem is that you are trying to make him into someone God doesn't want him to be,' he wisely advised her.

There followed several months of counselling for them both as a couple and as individuals. Andy and Linda had big changes to make in their attitudes to each other and in their general lifestyle. With the help of a couple of Christians who cared, Andy was able to sort out his relationship with God. He began to get his work-life in perspective. Even though rearranging his shift work to avoid Sundays meant a drop in salary, it was worth every penny because of the difference it made to their marriage to be able to worship together as a family. Encouraged in the realization that he did not have to live up to anyone else's image of him, except God's, Andy moved forward as a Christian, as a father and as a husband.

Linda needed to see how she had been (unconsciously) trying to make Andy into her version of a spiritual husband and father. She started to thank God for the husband he had given her, and moving on from this positive perspective she was able to look at the problems in their relationship in a new light. She began to see that an important dimension of Christian service she had totally overlooked was service to her husband. Changes needed to be made in her own outside commitments and, before many months, a very shaky marriage was up and sailing on a much more even keel.

## Growing together

Real-life people with real-life problems illustrate the point: marriages, even Christian ones, need to be worked at. There is hope for the toughest situation. God, who created marriage in the first place, is committed to help us make it work. As with everything in life there are responsibilities we need to shoulder and principles we must follow. The rest of this book seeks to explain and apply these responsibilities and principles. But before reading further, we need to answer with honesty a few questions. They make up the prerequisites for working at marriage. Whether you are already married or contemplating marriage, we suggest you think them over carefully, both personally and as a couple. Our responses are important, because they indicate where we stand in relation to our commitment to God as well as our commitment to our partner.

## Important questions

- Am I committed to God's will being done in my life?
- Am I willing to learn and apply the principles contained in the Bible concerning marriage as God intends it?
- Am I willing, by God's power, to make changes in my attitudes, ambitions, character and lifestyle?
- Am I willing to be totally honest about myself with myself and my partner?
- Am I prepared to receive honest, constructive criticism from my partner and, if necessary, responsible counsellors?
- Am I committed to making my marriage work, no matter what it costs or how long it takes?
- Am I prepared to express my commitment to my partner: 'For better, for worse, for richer, for poorer, in sickness and in health, to love and to cherish, till we are parted by death'?

One word recurs in these questions. It is the word *commitment*. It embodies God's attitude to marriage, which needs to be ours too if we want to discover the joy contained in one of the choicest gifts he has ever given.

## Notes

[1]Charles Swindoll, *Strike the Original Match* (Kingsway).

# CHAPTER TWO

# BUILDING
# YOUR MARRIAGE

The popular view of marriage is that it is like buying a brand-new car. On your wedding day you take ownership of this sparkling new thing we call marriage, in the same way that you would take delivery of a car from the showroom. It seems to us that some people have the idea that you spend the next forty years or so keeping at bay the ravages of time. New cars do not stay looking new for long. The paint loses its colour, the chrome goes dull and, as the miles increase, bits wear out or, worse still, drop off. The upholstery sags and tears, and rust eats its way into the once immaculate bodywork. The name of the game is to keep the car looking as good as you can for as long as possible but, as everyone knows, it will never look the way it did on the day it was delivered.

Is marriage something to be polished and patched up in the frustrating hope that we should try to keep it looking in mint condition?

Surely a more accurate picture is that of a do-it-yourself, self-assembly car kit. Your wedding day is the beginning of a lifetime of learning, building and creating something that will last. And much of the fulfilment comes in learning to put it together. In other words, a true Christian view of marriage has more to do with *building* than with *maintenance*. God wants to show us how to build a marriage that not only teaches us about his grace and kindness but will be a means of communicating his plans for the human race to those whose lives we touch.

The building of a marriage is a three-way partnership

involving a husband, a wife and God. Psalm 127 has been called 'the family psalm' because it deals with God's building plans for family life. Written by wise King Solomon, it was incorporated in the worship of the temple and provides a powerful reminder that, in building a marriage that lasts, God's help is indispensable:

> Unless the LORD builds the house,
>     its builders labour in vain.
> Unless the LORD watches over the city,
>     the watchmen stand guard in vain.
> In vain you rise early
>     and stay up late,
> toiling for food to eat –
>     for he grants sleep to those he loves.
>
> (Ps 127:1–2)

One of the most liberating concepts for any couple to grasp is that God is interested in the building of their marriage. All marriages face ups and downs, difficult decisions, good and bad times. God invites us to include him in every aspect of married life and to grow together in our knowledge of him.

When we were engaged to be married, we read Walter Trobisch's helpful book *I Married You.*[1] In it he repeats what we came to call the 'triangle principle' (see diagram). It helped us throughout the early years of marriage to remind ourselves of God's pattern for building. This simple picture has taught us some valuable lessons.

- *Jesus at the centre.* It is not 'my' marriage or 'our' marriage but God's marriage. It is in submission to his lordship that we find ourselves able to submit to each other.
- *Equal partners.* The Bible teaches that although there is a difference of *function* there is equality of *status* between husband and wife. We stand together before God on an equal footing, each responsible to him.

▶ *Growing together.* Trace your finger along the sides of the triangle. The closer we move towards Jesus Christ, the closer we come to each other. God wants us to enjoy maximum marriage, and the way to achieve it is through a closeness of walk together as disciples of Christ.

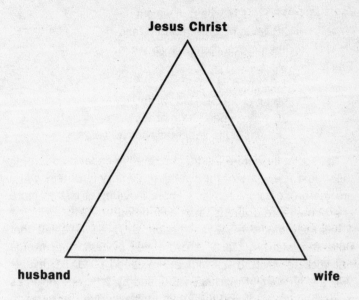

**God's building pattern for marriage**

Diagrams and principles seem impressive, but how do they work out in everyday life? Is a 'spiritual view' of marriage confined to an hour in church on a Sunday? How can we take the principles out of the classroom into the real world?

In order to answer these questions, we must face up to the fact that every marriage encounters pressures of different kinds. At a busy international airport the use of radar is essential in guiding a fully laden plane safely to the ground. We, too, need to be aware of the pressure points and hazards that confront marriages today.

## Some pressure points

Mr and Mrs Average Briton of the 1990s are an interesting couple to meet. He is:

> 1.75 m (5' 9") tall
> 78 kg (12st 4lbs) in weight
> 28 when he gets married, and
> his life expectancy is 75 years.

She is:

> 1.62 m (5' 4") tall
> 66 kg (10st 5lbs) in weight
> 26 years when she marries
> and has a life expectancy of 80 years.

The social indicators tell us of family life under pressure. In these last few years of the twentieth century in Britain, there are more one-parent families, more illegitimate births, more abortions, more divorces, than ever before.

A survey of the thirty-year period 1951–81 revealed that while the infant mortality rate dropped by 58%, the divorce rate rocketed by 338%. A look at the period 1971–91 reveals that the number of marriages dropped by 24% and divorces more than doubled, and the infant mortality rate continued to fall.[2] We may be growing in our knowledge of preserving life, but something appears to be missing in our search for quality of life.

From research it appears that the *pressure points* for most marriages centre on the following events.

*The first two to three years of marriage.* Adjustments to married life are not easy and most couples (if they are honest) will admit to tensions during their settling-in period. In a survey of our own, conducted anonymously with groups of newly-weds, the main difficulties encountered during the first few years were listed as learning to communicate with each other, adjusting to new responsibilities and financial problems.

*The arrival of the first baby.* As we shall discuss later (see chapter 8, 'Starting a family'), the arrival of a baby makes an enormous difference to a couple. Two becoming three means more than just another mouth to feed. It involves a total readjustment of life which takes time, patience and a lot of love from both partners.

*The wife's return to work.* The family budget inevitably causes many women to go out to work again once the children are at school. Often women stop work only to have a baby, and once maternity leave is completed they make arrangements to have the child cared for during working hours. Without discussing the pros and cons of this particular issue, we simply note that the wife recommencing work is cited as a pressure point in marriage. Strangely, although the additional income is seen as alleviating pressure, the extra demands on time sometimes produce additional burdens.

*The tenth year of marriage.* People often refer to the 'seven-year itch', but statistically divorce is more likely around the ten-year mark. The newness and novelty have worn off and possibly the arrival of children causes the partners to take the drastic step of divorce.

*Redundancy and long-term unemployment.* Without a doubt, the economic climate in many western nations in recent years has deeply affected family life. The shock of redundancy and the accompanying loss of self-esteem in an individual affect all family members. When a husband and father is suddenly at home all day with no prospect of immediate employment, the strain tells. When a job goes, it is more than income that is lost; a sense of purpose and value goes with it.

*Children leaving home.* Sadly, there are couples who stay together only 'for the sake of the children'. Once the children have grown up and left the nest, the motivation to keep the marriage going vanishes.

*Death of a close family member.* The death of a close relative or friend can have a devastating effect on a person.

Our western culture has no substantial grief pattern in which bereaved people can seek refuge. As a result, we do not cope with death in so honest a fashion as other societies. The death of someone close to us can effect a dramatic change in our personalities, and in some marriages the partners simply cannot handle the crisis.

*External problems.* Marriage soaks up pressures from all directions. There may be problems at work or in the neighbourhood. Close family or friends may be going through difficult times. All of this brings external pressure to a relationship.

*Retirement.* A major change of lifestyle always requires some getting used to. Retirement for one or both partners may have been a dream for years. But in reality there are big readjustments that must be made. Perhaps the routine of work and outside interests has papered over the cracks of relationship difficulties. When the regular pattern changes, the strains become all too apparent.

## Causes of marriage breakdown

What are the major causes of marriage breakdown? It must be realized that surveys and statistics are not always able to get to the root causes of a couple's inability to work at marriage together. But the main contributing factors to breakdown appear to be the following.

*Lack of communication.* From our own experience, as well as counselling other couples, it is obvious that breaking the sound barrier in marriage is a complex problem which some people never achieve. If a couple cannot learn to communicate with each other it will add strains which the relationship may not be able to bear.

*Sexual problems.* In a so-called age of enlightenment when books abound on the subject, it seems that many couples experience real incompatibility in an area that God designed for maximum enjoyment.

*Money and housing difficulties.* Lack of money or problems with housing are cited as a major cause of breakdown in marriage. Pressures such as having a mortgage greater than the value of your house, or working on short-term contracts, seem great. But for some people the problem is not having a house or a job to start with! Admittedly, compared with our grandparents, we have much more going for us from a material point of view, but easier divorce laws mean that our will to fight together against the economic odds is not as strong as it used to be.

*Jealousy.* It is sobering to recognize that something the Bible repeatedly warns us about is cited as a cause of marriage breakdown. Heart attitudes always affect behaviour patterns. Jealousy need not be focused upon another person seen as a threat to a relationship. You can be jealous of your partner's job success or even his or her looks!

*Isolation.* Marriage was designed in part to provide mutual companionship. How sad to realize that for some it is a painfully lonely experience. Feeling the loss of independence, some couples find themselves trapped in a prison of loneliness.

*Violence.* Battered wives, battered children and even cases of battered husbands feature in our newspapers regularly. Some argue that the problem has always existed, and it is only the development of media interest that has brought it into the open. Like it or not, violence in the home is a startling symptom of a sick society. Ungoverned tempers do more than bruise bodies; they break marriages.

*Immaturity.* Some people are honest enough to admit that their marriage failed because one partner (or both) was too immature to cope with the adjustments needed to build a successful relationship. Incidentally, maturity has little to do with age. Teenage marriages can work, and similarly a couple of newly-weds in their thirties can prove to be as immature in their attitudes as children in a playgroup.

*Adultery.* Soap-opera morality has done much to popularize adultery. In an age of 'Kleenex' relationships (use one and throw it away), an extramarital 'fling' is regarded as normal. But not many marriages can survive the awful legacy of a broken commitment. Open marriage may be popular in some circles but it certainly is not practical when it comes to building strong relationships.

Being aware of the pressure points is vital for building a marriage that will last. You have probably been able to identify a number of them already. We certainly have found it helpful to realize that we are not alone in the problems we face.

But there are special pressures on a couple determined to go God's way. We have given a brief summary of the secular scene, but it seems to us that Christian marriages face peculiar difficulties and tensions. From our own married life, plus scores of discussions with other Christian couples, we have highlighted five danger areas.

## Christian marriages under fire

### Spiritual warfare

Christian marriages are under attack in the spiritual warfare that rages around us. C. S. Lewis, in his Preface to *The Screwtape Letters,*[3] warns of the twin dangers that Christians face whenever we talk about the devil. One is to ignore him totally and to dismiss the idea of any personification of evil as primitive superstition. The other danger is to see Satan everywhere and to be totally trapped in the fatalistic belief that he is behind everything that goes wrong in our lives.

With this wise caution in mind we believe that there is a wholesale satanic onslaught against the Christian family. We have only to look at the alarming increase of marriage breakdown among Christian leaders to support this claim. Churches of all denominations throughout Europe and North

America have been rocked by marriages of Christian leaders that have been wrecked.

The Bible exhorts us to 'put on the full armour of God so that you can take your stand against the devil's schemes' (Eph. 6:11). Without a doubt, part of the devil's scheme is to attack any marriage relationship where there is a determination to put Jesus Christ at the centre. This should not make us paranoid, but instead help us to understand that some of the problems we encounter are simply due to the fact that we are involved in a war. Going God's way together is the most sure defence against such attacks.

## Ignorance

As Christians we can sometimes be painfully thick and naïve. And we (the authors) point the finger at ourselves as much as anyone when we make that statement, because we have learned the truth of it the hard way. Without detracting from what we have just said about the spiritual battle, some of us do need to understand that building a Christian marriage involves more than hymns and prayers. Here are just a few examples of where ignorance needs to be overcome.

*Marriage needs to be worked at.* Being two committed Christians does not excuse us from the sweat and slog of working on our relationship together. Marriages made in heaven still need to be worked out on earth. This book explores ways in which we can tackle this.

*Compartmental Christianity.* We pigeon-hole our lives into 'spiritual bits' and 'other things'. Learning about the totality of life as Christians is important for our healthy development as human beings. Being a Christian couple means more than going to church together. It involves learning to 'think Christianly' about every aspect of married life: how we spend our money, our attitude towards our home and possessions, our ambitions and dreams, how we are learning to give as well as take. All these and more help us move towards an understanding of what it means to involve God in every part of our lives together.

*Sexual enjoyment in marriage.* Christians can sometimes be repressed people. Hang-ups from the past need to be faced and overcome, skeletons removed from the closet and unhelpful attitudes corrected. God is not against sex; he created it. The enjoyment of each other's bodies within the bond of marriage is not dirty but a beautiful gift which can teach us much about God. Ignorance of human sexuality has created many unnecessary problems for Christian couples, who are held back from discovering the fulfilment that this marvellous gift from God can bring. Some of us carry into marriage sexual experiences from previous relationships; these may not have helped us in growing into a healthy view of sexuality, and we need to be prepared to make some changes in our attitudes.

*Refusal to admit problems.* We may have been brought up to believe the statement, 'Christians don't have any problems in marriage.' If you accept that, you have sentenced yourselves to a lifetime of disillusionment and despair. Every couple, Christian or not, needs to learn how to be good marriage partners. And the learning process involves making mistakes. One young couple wrote to us during the writing of this book, pleading for practical realism. They asked for help in adjusting to married life and the encouragement of 'just knowing that other people have experienced the same difficulties'.

## Imbalance

All of us, in some measure, suffer from lack of balance in our Christian lives. We may be over-involved in our local church, or equally the problem may be that we are not involved enough. Getting the right balance between work, home and church responsibilities seems to be a widespread difficulty. Every couple will face the constant pressure of getting a right balance in their personal lives, but for Christians the problem is compounded by our involvement in a local church.

We can easily become trapped in a busy round of activities that leave us with little or no time to develop our relationship together. Too often the option taken is to step back from being involved in our local church, which then presents problems of a different kind as we become spiritually dried out and rootless. It is important to develop 'quality time' – in other words, making the most of the time you spend together. We have found that this is something that needs constant re-evaluation as circumstances change. A pattern which may be ideal before children arrive will need to be amended to fit in with the demands of a growing family. Fighting for balance is a constant battle – but worth every ounce of effort.

## The see-saw syndrome

The difficulties posed where one partner is a Christian and the other is not are dealt with later in the book (see chapter 5, 'Partners with God'). But the 'see-saw syndrome', as we will call it, has many similarities.

In a marriage you sometimes find one partner who is a committed Christian with a deep desire to follow Jesus Christ in every area of life, whereas the other, although a Christian, is not moving forward in his or her walk with God. Like two children on a see-saw, you have the tension of imbalance as a continual pressure point.

There are no easy answers, but from our own experience, patience, love, prayer and honesty are indispensable assets in a relationship where one is spiritually further on than his or her partner. One word of caution: beware of harsh judgments. Be wary of comparing your partner with someone you see as the perfect picture of an 'ideal' Christian. This is unhelpful for a growing marriage relationship, and it is also unrealistic. Believe it or not, that 'ideal' person has a list of weaknesses if you look closely enough! Allowing God to show us how he sees our partner's progress is a good antidote to the problem.

## Close-up fellowship

Thank God that in recent years many churches have moved on to a deeper understanding of what Christian fellowship means. 'God's frozen chosen' have gradually been thawing out – and about time too! But if you belong to a church where hugs have replaced handshakes as the standard Christian greeting you will perhaps be aware of the attendant dangers. A renewed emphasis on holy hugs and kisses, shared lifestyles and close fellowship has created some real tensions. A much-respected older minister once asked us if we knew the difference between a kiss and the 'holy kiss' which Scripture encourages us to practise. Expecting some deeply theological answer, we failed to notice the twinkle in his eye. 'About one minute forty-seven seconds,' he explained.

Behind the humour lies an important point. Brotherly and sisterly fellowship is helpful and to be encouraged. But we must never forget our own sinful nature or that of those we have fellowship with. There is a difference between hugging and groping, and one-to-one late-night counselling sessions can produce more problems than solutions.

We have learned through the years that unless couples and churches have clearly defined codes of conduct all sorts of problems occur. And the time to lay down the guidelines is before a situation arises.

On a trip to the USA Ian stopped to fill the car with petrol. In this out-in-the-sticks place there were no rest rooms (toilets) and he asked to use the staff facility. On the wall of the washroom was a startling poster: 'What to do in the event of a hold-up'. Listed beneath (with graphic illustrations) were instructions to employees about the exact procedure to be followed if they should ever find themselves looking down the wrong end of a gun barrel. Forewarned is forearmed. And if we are aware of some of the pressures we are likely to face we will be better equipped to deal with them.

## Four strong pillars

To build a marriage that lasts we need a firm foundation. Paul tells the Corinthians, 'For no-one can lay any foundation other than the one already laid, which is Jesus Christ' (1 Cor. 3:11). Peter speaks of Jesus as 'the living Stone – rejected by men but chosen by God and precious to him' (1 Pet. 2:4).

There is no better foundation for marriage than the Lord Jesus Christ himself. That is why it is so important for a couple thinking about marriage to discover where they both stand in relation to the Christian faith. Following Christ is not an activity on the level of an outside interest, but a relationship which affects the whole fabric of our lives. To be united in faith and commitment to Jesus is the most secure foundation any marriage can find. Of course, marriages where one partner is not a committed Christian (or even where both are not) can and do work successfully. But in order to discover the Creator's best for our lives, we need, individually and as a couple, to be in a right relationship with him. God has made this possible for us through the life, death and resurrection of his Son, Jesus Christ. 'For there is one God and one mediator between God and men, the man Christ Jesus, who gave himself as a ransom for all men' (1 Tim. 2:5–6). Building on the foundation of a personal relationship with God through Christ is part of the adventure of Christian marriage.

A solid marriage relationship has four dimensions, we believe. Through the rest of this book we shall be discussing the areas of married life that each dimension encompasses. We like to think of them as pillars. Pillars take the weight, bear the strain and provide the support on which you can build. These four pillars are interlinked; none is of greater or lesser importance than any of the others. Concentrating on building each of them strongly is the only way we know to develop a healthy, balanced marriage.

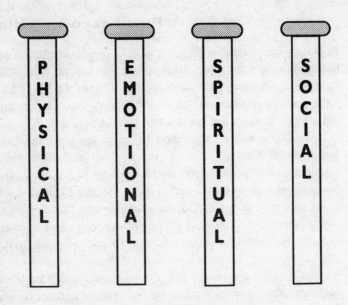

**Four pillars for building a strong marriage**

In describing these four dimensions of marriage, we do not list them in any particular order of importance. Each is integral to the others, but defining them helps us to discover areas where our marriage may need strengthening.

## 1. Physical – making love

The physical dimension of marriage is important, though not all-important. Erotic love is nothing to be ashamed of; it is part of God's wonderful creation plan, and the sexual intimacy of a marriage relationship is a very special gift to be enjoyed.

The phrase 'making love' is a very good description of what a sexual relationship is meant to achieve. Physical closeness, touching and caressing are ways in which we can actually make or build a deeper love relationship with our partner. The physical dimension covers more than the act of sexual intercourse. Holding hands, an affectionate kiss and cuddling are all ways in which we can express our love for each other. Every partnership is different. Some couples are excessively demonstrative while others do not seem to have the same need to be constantly in each other's arms. There is nothing worse than trying to play your own game to someone else's rules. That is why it is important to learn early on in your marriage to be honest with each other and sensitive to your partner's needs.

Perhaps men (due to their psychological make-up) are the worst culprits here. Later (in chapter 6, 'Loving and learning') we shall talk about learning to understand each other, but it is worth mentioning now that building the physical pillar of your marriage means much more than having sex as often as you want to.

Touching, kissing and holding are important ways to reassure and affirm your partner. It is a whole way of life that should not end with the honeymoon but continue to be cultivated as your marriage deepens. The sexual relationship between a couple is not meant to lessen as years go by, but to grow deeper and richer.

We are willing to confess (although we never admitted it to each other) that we both believed that, sexually, marriage started on a 'high' and gradually dwindled with the passing of time. For those who have shared painful and difficult experiences on their honeymoon it must have been depressing to think, 'This can only get worse!' The truth is that twenty-something years on and four children later we can only admit (with breathless enthusiasm!) that it gets better all the time. Every couple will experience times when the physical side of their relationship goes through difficulties. Pregnancy, the menstrual cycle, pressures at work and broken nights with teething babies all combine to attack the physical enjoyment of each other. But perseverance, understanding and a healthy sense of humour will help you work through those patches.

We once heard a lecture by a learned man of God who said, 'You begin to make love to your partner not in the bedroom at night but at the breakfast table in the morning.' Checking that we had not misheard the revered gentleman saying 'on the breakfast table', we took the advice to heart. Building a good physical relationship together involves more than what happens in the bedroom; it means the expression of love in a thousand ways beyond words.

## 2. Emotional – making love go deeper

God ordained marriage for a number of important reasons:

- *Procreation:* the birth of children
- *Physical intimacy:* the enjoyment of sexual love in a committed relationship
- *Social stability:* the fabric of society is strong when marriage and family life are strong
- *Friendship:* so that instead of being alone, people may discover fellowship at its deepest level

Companionship is an old-fashioned word but it addresses a very modern need. Marriage is meant to be a place of friendship, where two people can grow together in a deep bond of emotional security. It is a neglected area of marriage, not least because of the communication breakdown from which many couples suffer.

For too many of us, after the wedding, communication goes no deeper than talking about superficial, everyday things. Some never learned how to communicate before they were married, and have not changed much since. Communicating with each other is a vital skill that must be developed if we are going to grow together.

Growing strong emotionally also means learning to share

life at all levels. A friend is someone you enjoy being with. Is your marriage partner your best friend or, putting it another way, do you want him or her to become your best friend?

Learning how to live together is an exciting business, but it takes time. It involves a good deal of give and take. It may mean standing on the terraces freezing to death alongside him, or giving the match a miss in order to go shopping alongside her. But if you are going to grow together emotionally it takes more than reading a book; it takes time – not time wasted but time invested.

One of the frustrations we encountered in the early years of marriage was the fact that we were involved in full-time Christian ministry. It is a privilege to be called by God into ministry, but an attendant danger is that you become totally absorbed in Christian work and very detached from the real world. We made it a policy early on in our marriage to 'break out' as often as possible. It sometimes meant a night at the theatre or cinema, going to watch the greatest team in London play football, or else to find a quiet pub or restaurant where we could just talk: sport, politics, art, fashion – anything that would help us maintain a proper perspective on life and each other.

Within six weeks of getting married we made one of the most important investments in our married life: a chocolate-brown mongrel dog we named Mr Russell, purchased for £5 from a market stall in London's East End. A dog needs daily exercise, and that guaranteed that both of us could walk out together at regular intervals each week. Looking back, we believe the hours spent walking Russ were some of the most valuable times together in our early years. Give yourselves time and space to grow together emotionally.

## 3. Spiritual – growing together in God

The third pillar is the spiritual dimension of marriage. This does not mean that God is excluded from the other three!

Building a balanced relationship involves giving special attention to growing together in God.

When a couple get married, they do not cease to exist as individuals before God. We need a personal walk with him as well as a shared spiritual experience. From conversations with many friends it is apparent that this is an area which causes some concern. For instance, a couple may find it easy to pray and read the Bible on their own but far more difficult to do the same things in the presence of the other. Some find the reverse to be true; they enjoy joint prayer but find it difficult to maintain a personal devotional life. It is all too easy to get caught up in the trap of guilt and self-condemnation. What may be right for another couple might not be any help to you. The important thing is that you are both growing together in God and feel able to share openly with each other about the deep things of the heart.

There are certain guidelines which we have learned about growing together spiritually.

*Pray together.* It is important to develop a personal prayer life, but learning the discipline of praying together is a means of strengthening your marriage. We have discovered that as family life changes so our pattern of prayer together has altered. Learn to begin and end each day in prayer. Bring all the decisions you make together to God in prayer. Some of our most realistic prayer times have been when we've sat down to work out the monthly budget!

*Read the Word of God together.* Again, the arrival of children may mean adapting your pattern. Nowadays, we find ourselves ploughing through the varied delights of children's Bible-reading notes in a family prayer time. But during the early years of marriage, we tried to make time to read the Bible and pray at the end of our evening meal on a regular basis.

*Worship together.* We believe that being committed to a local Christian church where the Word of God is taught is vital for building a strong Christian marriage. There are exceptional cases when God specifically calls people to a situation where there are no other Christians, but even in such instances the couple concerned need the support of other believers. Setting commitment to a local church high on your priority list will help your growth in the spiritual dimension of your marriage.

*Serving together.* If your view of church is like that of the local take-away you will not progress far as Christians. Being part of God's church in his world means service. Serving together may involve a role you can both undertake, but not necessarily. Do not hold out for a joint job with your church, because that may not be God's plan for you at this stage. Determine to be involved together in serving God where he has put you.

*Giving together.* Joint finances mean a re-evaluation of your Christian giving. One way in which you can include God more fully in your married life together is by your financial commitment to his work.

One last word of advice about growing together spiritually: Be yourselves! We recently had a meal in a home where it was obvious that the family were on their best behaviour. Everyone looked strained, and the children's programmes on TV were firmly switched off as the family stereo boomed out the latest praise and worship album. We felt thoroughly uncomfortable until it dawned on us that these kind people believed this was the sort of 'spiritual atmosphere' in which we would feel most comfortable. We soon put them straight! Learning to be natually spiritual and spiritually natural will help others to see Jesus far more easily than if we pretend to be something that we are not.

## 4. Social – reaching out to others

One of the arguments put forward by those who oppose the idea of the traditional family unit in favour of open-ended relationships is that the nuclear family is a selfish concept, doomed to extinction. It's a case of little people living in little boxes each failing to relate to anything except on the most superficial level, and doing little to meet real needs around them.

But is the family meant to be a self-contained unit? Is marriage a castle in which we hide ourselves away, having pulled up the drawbridge? A truly Christian marriage must have a soial dimension to it if it is going to reflect God's care and compassion for people. To develop this area of marriage we need to look beyond our own immediate families. It is not just the Italian Mafia who have godfathers; ordinary families have their fair share, plus a few godmothers as well. We have been amazed in writing this book to discover how many young couples experience interference from parents, in-laws and other relatives.

You do not have to live under anyone's domination or control except that of Jesus Christ. His opinion is far more important than anyone else's. One way to establish the social pillar in your marriage is to develop friendships as a couple. Neighbours or members of your church are the most obvious people to start with. But include non-Christians in your circle. We have met hundreds of people who have come to a personal faith in Jesus through Christian couples opening their homes. Also, determine to broaden your circle of contacts beyond other young marrieds. Single people, students and the elderly all need to have a home open to them.

Four words sum up the ministry of a Christian home:

- *Healing:* a place where hurt people find security, love and acceptance.
- *Hospitality:* a neglected spiritual gift which, when used, enables God to reach and bless people.
- *Hope:* people who have been damaged through the trauma of a marriage break-up or who have been victims of abuse can recover confidence in marriage and family life.

▶ *Happiness:* there is a special joy in being part of a family. Learning to share that joy with others is part of our Christian responsibility.

Concentrating on the social dimension of your marriage also involves building bridges out from your home as well as into it. Getting involved in your community is much easier before children start to arrive, but even then natural opportunities arise through parent-teacher associations and the like. Even an involvement together in a regular sports activity such as squash or badminton is a valuable way to develop together socially as a couple.

Four important pillars: physical, emotional, spiritual and social. Over the next few chapters we shall be looking in more detail at how we strengthen these areas of our relationship. We said at the start of this book that there are no experts in marriage, only learners. These four pillars need looking at constantly throughout marriage to see how they can be developed and strengthened.

Building a strong marriage together with God is not a purely selfish pursuit. It is part of God's means to bless society as a whole. The German theologian Dietrich Bonhoeffer touched on this when he wrote to his niece on the eve of her wedding:

Marriage is more than your love for each other. It has a higher dignity and power for it is God's holy ordinance through which He wills to perpetuate the human race until the end of time. In your love you see only your two selves in the world, but in your marriage you are a link in the chain of the generations; which God causes to come and to pass away to His glory and calls into His Kingdom. In your love you see only the heaven of your happiness but in marriage you are placed at a post of responsibility towards the world and mankind. Your love is your own private possession but marriage is more than something personal – it is a status, an office.[4]

## Notes

1. Walter Trobisch, *I Married You* (IVP).
2. *Social Trends* (Central Statistical Office, December 1995).
3. C. S. Lewis, *The Screwtape Letters* (Fontana).
4. Quoted in Larry Christensen, *The Christian Family* (Fountain Trust), p. 9.

# CHAPTER THREE

# TWO INTO ONE

A man was walking on a deserted beach when he noticed a strange-looking object protruding from a sand dune. Moving closer he saw it was an old Prussian-style military helmet, the type with a large spike sticking up in the centre. Thinking his find would make a good ornament, he bent down to pick it up. As he did so, an agonized scream came from underneath the helmet and a man's head (wearing the helmet) popped out of the sand. 'Thank goodness you've come,' puffed the owner of the helmet (and the head). 'I've been here ages. Can you pull me out? I'm stuck!'

After several minutes of digging, the top part of the soldier's body was freed from the sand. But no matter how hard the man tugged and pushed he could not free the unfortunate prisoner. Exhausted and perspiring, he collapsed on the sand alongside the soldier. 'It's no good,' he gasped. 'I can't shift you. I'll have to go and get some help.'

'Please don't leave me,' the soldier pleaded. 'Look, give me one more really hard pull. Tell you what, though,' he said thoughtfully, 'would it help if I took my feet out of the stirrups first?'

Problems often turn out to be bigger than we imagined. Like the man on the beach we sometimes find ourselves tackling situations too big to manage by ourselves. Not long into married life you will discover problems that will need your attention. Tensions and difficulties occur even in the closest relationships, and part of the process of building a strong marriage is learning to work through them together.

*Adjustment* is an important word for the early years of marriage. It describes the process of two individuals, who have lived relatively independent lives, working now at living together. It means getting used to sharing a bed with another person, and coping with new responsibilities such as cooking and running a home. It involves learning how to manage money and plan your time, taking someone else's plans into account. At times the adjustment process can be fun, but it can also be frustrating. In this chapter we are going to look at some of the adjustments that need to be made in the early years of marriage and consider the attitudes that will help to make them work.

## You'll never walk alone

In preparing to write this book we conducted an anonymous survey with quite a wide variety of Christian couples. One of the questions that we asked was, 'In which areas did you experience difficulties in adjusting to married life?'

---

### ADJUSTMENTS IN MARRIAGE

**List in order the five main areas of adjustment you have faced**

1.

2.

3.

4.

5.

---

Before we give you the answers, why not test yourself? Using the box, list the five major adjustment areas you have faced as a couple. If you are not married yet, then look ahead and try to predict where these pressures will come.

Now compare your experience with that of other couples. From our survey the following Top Five emerged.

1  Learning to communicate with each other
2  Adjusting to financial responsibilities and running a home
3  Overcoming difficulties in sexual relations
4  Interference from parents
5  Organizing time properly

You may be able to identify with some of the things mentioned on the list. If you can, be encouraged to realize you are not alone! Many of the couples questioned had success- fully worked through those difficult months of adjustment. You are not in any way unusual in the tensions you find yourself facing, and learning to overcome them will make your relationship stronger in the long run.

We have already mentioned that God is committed to making your relationship work. If you are prepared to make the changes as he directs, then you will discover his help in the nitty-gritty business of two individuals becoming one.

## Side by side

In our own experience we have learned that there are five steps in the adjustment process.

*1. Identify the problem.* What is causing the tension? It may be the inability to make the housekeeping money last the month, or your untidiness in leaving clothes on the floor. Whatever it is, identify the cause together. No problem is too small to qualify!

*2. Discuss your feelings.* Don't ignore the issue, because

that will not solve the problem. You need to sit down together and have an honest chat. It can be easy for 'honest' chats to develop into full-blown rows, so make sure you are prepared to *listen* to your partner's point of view as well as expressing your own opinion.

*3. Pray.* Prayer is not just something we do only when we feel like it. God invites us to share our concerns with him at all times. Ask for his help in adjusting to each other. What you are discussing may not seem a very 'spiritual' thing to pray about. But pray anyway, because by so doing you are including God in your lives (see Pr. 3:5–6).

*4. Agree on a course of action.* Both of you need to make adjustments, and it is good to agree together on what action needs to be taken. To give a personal example, one of the areas of tension for us in our first year or so of marriage related to finance. Having allocated the month's house-keeping, we found that within two weeks it had usually all gone! We reached a mutual agreement that we needed to decide on a monthly budget for housekeeping. We also agreed that we would stick with that figure and check it weekly as the month progressed. With a little time and planning we found we were surviving each month with a few pounds to spare. It was a very simple solution (why didn't we think of it earlier?) to what had become an area of disagreement.

*5. Re-evaluate the situation.* Look at things again after a month or so and discuss how you feel about the course of action you decided to take. You may find it necessary to make changes in the light of what has happened.

The first years of married life are going to make demands on you both. You will need to have patience with each other, particularly as you begin to realize that your partner is not as perfect as you imagined him or her to be before your wedding. Remember, your partner has been discovering that you are not perfect either! Here is a situation where you can practise grace and forgiveness. And remember, use a lot of love, which is the cement that makes relationships strong.

We turn now to some specific adjustments husbands and wives need to make as they start out on married life. You will probably find it helpful to read your partner's section as well as your own, in order to get a more balanced picture.

## Adjustments men need to make

As individuals, we are all different. That is why it is difficult to make sweeping generalizations. What may be good advice for one person may be quite unnecessary for someone else. With that caution in mind, we would highlight the following main areas where most Christian men find that adjustments are needed in the early years of marriage.

### Learning to take responsibility

Ephesians 5:25–30 makes challenging reading for any Christian husband:

> Husbands, love your wives, just as Christ loved the church and gave himself up for her to make her holy, cleansing her by the washing with water through the word, and to present her to himself as a radiant church, without stain or wrinkle or any other blemish, but holy and blameless. In this same way, husbands ought to love their wives as their own bodies. He who loves his wife loves himself. After all, no-one ever hated his own body, but he feeds and cares for it, just as Christ does the church – for we are members of his body.

God equates a husband's care for his wife with Christ's love for the church. How does Christ love his church?

- *Realistically:* he does not wait for us to be good enough to qualify for his love. It is a love without conditions, hating sin but loving the sinner.
- *Sacrificially:* he gave up his life on our behalf. Forgiveness came

at his expense, not ours. Jesus' sacrifice of self-interest brought salvation to us.

- *Redemptively:* it was to make us clean, holy and whole people that Christ died. His desire is that we should be without stain, wrinkle or blemish.
- *Pastorally:* Christ cares for his people. He feeds them and cares for them as a shepherd looks after his flock. His concern is our well-being, security and growth.

Take those four words: realistically, sacrificially, redemptively, pastorally. They sum up God's pattern for a husband. It is a high standard to follow, but God has promised his help to fulfil the conditions.

God has invested spiritual authority in the husband as the family head, but that authority is to be exercised with love. We face two dangerous extremes when it comes to authority within marriage.

First, some men fail to take any authority. Possibly your mother was a single parent who brought you up alone. This may mean that she became the chief decision-maker and, in the early years, she organized your life to some degree. Be very careful that you don't sit back and allow your wife to become a substitute for your mum. Laziness is more of a male character defect than a female one and, unless you check yourself, you will find you have let your responsibilities slide.

Second, some men go overboard on authority. God wants you to be a pastoral leader, not a military dictator. You are not commanding a battleship but seeking, with God's help, to build a home. True spiritual authority comes through serving others. The lower you stoop, the taller you grow, is a principle of God's kingdom. Keep those five words from Ephesians in front of you: *as Christ loved the church.* That is how you are to love your wife.

If you take proper responsibility for your wife within your marriage relationship it will be evident in a number of ways.

- You will pray for her on a regular (*i.e.* daily) basis.
- You will show interest in and concern for her spiritual development.
- You will take the lead in suggesting regular opportunities for prayer, Bible study and sharing together.
- You will be concerned about her development as a person.
- You will want to spend time with her, because the more you delight in her, the more of a delight she becomes to you.
- You will always be looking for ways to enrich, encourage and bless her.

Perhaps those ideals seem lofty, but like all ideals they are well worth pursuing.

## Getting your priorities straight

Here is an equation worth learning:

$$Singleness = independence$$
$$Marriage = interdependence$$

*Independence* sums up a single person's lifestyle. Within reason, you can eat when you like, go to bed when you like, map out your own leisure time and choose when you want to be with people. When you embark on married life the independence suddenly becomes *interdependence*, and you have to adjust to another person's presence in your life. Quite a number of couples refer to the strange feeling of having another person around most of the time. It certainly takes getting used to!

Instead of thinking 'single' you need to learn to think 'double' and alter your priorities accordingly. We know of relationships where all marriage has meant to the man is a change of address, someone else to do the washing, a regular sex life, full stop. Their social life, spending habits and the like have remained just as they were when they were single. You have another person to take into account, and you need to adjust your decision-making process to include your partner. She has an opinion that matters, and the right to express it and be heard.

Another way in which you can practise interdependence is by sharing the tasks of running your home. Most newly-weds (if they both have full-time jobs) find it difficult to cope with the demands of running a home. Cooking, shopping, cleaning and fixing things that go wrong all take time. If you leave these tasks to your wife you are not really shouldering your responsibilities properly. Work out some of the ways in which you can play your part in being a true partner in the home.

## Leaving and cleaving

The first reference to marriage in the Bible comes, as you would expect, in Genesis, in the creation account. Genesis 2:24 contains a principle that is repeated several times in Scripture, and on one occasion at least by Jesus himself: 'For this reason a man will leave his father and mother and be united to his wife, and they will become one flesh' (Gn. 2:24).

It has always puzzled us why it refers to a man leaving his parents with no mention of the woman leaving hers! One reason, perhaps, is seen in the cultural custom of a woman leaving the security of her parents and coming under the protection of her husband. But the man is expected to leave his parents to create a secure home and family of his own. The Scripture makes two things clear: the man is to *leave* his home and *cleave* to his wife.

Leaving and cleaving are important elements of starting out in marriage. As a man, it is possible to leave home physically while remaining there emotionally. If you are going to grow in your new relationship within marriage then you need to cut the ties with home. When a new baby comes into the world, it is still attached to the mother by the umbilical cord. Within minutes of birth the cord is cut. It does not lessen the relationship between mother and child but it moves that child forward into a new stage of life. The mark of the umbilical cord will remain on the growing child's body through into adulthood and old age – the indelible reminder of the joining that once bound mother and child. But for full development to take place, the cord, which for those early months within the womb had been the life-preserver, must be cut for ever.

Your links with your parents will not lessen as you leave home, but you must accept that your relationship with them has changed. We were amazed at how high on the adjustments list (see p. 53) interference from parents scored. But from subsequent counselling situations we have discovered many men who have not yet crossed the hurdle of leaving home emotionally.

It does not mean that you should be rude to your parents but it may mean being firm with them. It does not mean banning them from visiting your home, but if they are creating tensions between you as a couple it may mean limiting the visits. God does not want you to despise your parents or forget how much they have given to you, but he may want you to be honest with them about the level of involvement they can reasonably expect to have in your marriage. It doesn't mean ignoring their advice, but you do need to make it clear that you now have to take your own decisions. Finally, 'leaving and cleaving' certainly does not mean neglecting your parents; quite the opposite. We are positively commanded in Scripture to provide for them and honour them. But you may need to make your new priorities clear to them.

### Keeping your wife beautiful

How your wife looks is a reflection of how you love her. If she looks a mess, the chances are that that is how you treat her. A few pages back we quoted the verse in Ephesians which says: 'Husbands ought to love their wives as their own bodies' (Eph. 5:28). Most of us (unless we have a deep problem of self-image) take care of ourselves and pay some attention to how we look, and what we wear. We are to care for our wives in this way too.

Words are very important to women; more so than to a man. Make sure you build your partner up by complimenting her on her appearance, saying 'thank you' for a good meal, noticing small things and commenting on them appreciatively. Helping her to choose clothes, allowing her to express her personality through dress, hairstyle and make-up – all these things help to affirm her as a person.

Not too far into married life you will soon learn to read one another's signals. These are the signs we give out which indicate how we are feeling. Learn to read those signals and pay attention to them. You will soon discover how to step in and help your wife when she is feeling tired, under pressure about something that is worrying her or just needing to have a good talk.

Compliments, warm words and time alone are not just for courtship days. Carry them over into your marriage and you will be an enriched couple. Surprise presents, bouquets of flowers and love letters are a few examples of how some men help to build up their partner as a person and keep romance alive in their relationship.

## Sexual adjustment

Men and women are different not just in their bodies but also in their emotional and mental responses. This is seen very clearly within the sexual relationship. The sex act for a man is something he can do relatively quickly. For a woman, preparation and proper build-up are essential. You need to begin to learn how your wife can respond to you physically, and she needs to make discoveries about your responsiveness too.

To help you in this area of adjustment, here are some basic ground rules to help you develop a healthy sexual relationship together.

*Don't rush.* Rome was not built in a day, and neither was romance. You will not achieve deep sexual fulfilment for some time. Like riding a bike, good sex takes practice; but it is more fun learning about sex and it's less painful than falling off a bike! Believe it or not, most couples find that their sex life improves as time goes on, so be prepared to be patient.

Learn to please your partner, not just yourself. It is very easy to be selfish about sex. 'How often?' is a question that only the two of you can work out together, but learn to give as well as take.

*Communicate.* Most sexual difficulties in marriage can actually be talked through if both partners are willing to listen to each other. Spend time discovering how your partner feels about things. Also, learn to use words in your love-making. Your partner needs to *hear* that she is loved, and soft words can have as romantic an impact as sweet music and low lights.

Recently we talked to a couple one of whose main difficulties in marriage was the fact that the man made love in total silence. The clinical atmosphere was killing the relationship and the woman was the sort of person who desperately needed to be reassured, affirmed and built up. Instead, the silence reinforced all her feelings of inadequacy. Learn to communicate and, even though at first you feel uncomfortable about it, you will discover, as time goes on, that it becomes easier and more natural.

## Adjustments women need to make

Probably the most dramatic social changes in western society in the twentieth century have been among women. We may still have a long way to go in the equality stakes, but we have travelled quite a distance from where we started. But, in turn, that has created new pressures. Adjusting to being a wife today is *different* from your grandmother's experience, but that does not mean it is any easier.

We have already seen what Ephesians 5 has to say about husbands and their responsibility to love their wives. The biblical instruction for wives is not as detailed as it is for men, but it is equally direct: 'Wives, submit to your husbands as to the Lord ... Now as the church submits to Christ, so also wives should submit to their husbands in everything' (Eph. 5:22, 24).

'Submission' is a word that can easily be misunderstood and wrongly applied. It does *not* mean dumb obedience, the suppression of personality or doing as you are told irrespective of your opinion. In our view (though there are different ways of understanding Paul's words), it *does* mean recognizing the God-appointed order for family life. Submission means giving respect and trust to your partner. After all, if a man is loving his wife in the same way that Jesus loves the church, submitting to his protective, caring leadership will not be a difficult thing to do.

Notice the verses immediately before the section on family life in Ephesians 5. We are told to live as children of light (v. 8), and to live as wise people in an evil world (v. 15). To do this we are encouraged to 'be filled with the Spirit' (v. 18). This will flow out in a balanced life of worship and joy (v. 19) and it will also be seen in the way we submit to each other out of our love for Jesus Christ (v. 21). It is in this context that God's pattern for husbands and wives, parents and children, masters and servants is given (Eph. 5:22 – 6:9).

It is dangerous to pick out one verse in isolation. We are called to live Spirit-filled lives that affect our attitudes in all our relationships. That includes marriage, and without God's help we cannot be the wife or husband he wants us to be.

What are some of the adjustments that a woman needs to make as she sets out on married life?

## One life, two jobs

If you decide (as most women do) to carry on working as you settle into married life, you will quickly discover that you have multiplied your workload without increasing the number of hours in each day. Running a home, planning meals, shopping, washing and ironing, cleaning: all take time and you will find yourself constantly fighting to find an extra few minutes in the day to get another job done. It can lead to frustration, tiredness and arguments. How can you get to grips with these new responsibilities?

*Plan your time.* Plan your time at the start of each week. List the priorities and allocate specific times to tackle jobs. Don't just let things happen, plan them.

*Share the responsibilities.* Even the most macho male is liberated enough to flick a duster over the furniture! If you have decided that it is right to continue with a full-time job then it is only fair that you reach an agreement on dividing responsibilities in running the home. Talk it through and decide on a plan of action.

*Maintain a balance.* You may need to cut out some outside activities if you find you are not able to cope with your new responsibilities. It is no use being a busy, active Christian worker in your local church if your home is a tip and your marriage is falling apart because of your lack of practical care. If you plan your time properly you will be able to strike a balance which will help you to fit in everything that it is right for you to be involved with.

*Plan time off.* If you are always up and about, working from early morning to late at night, the stress will show in other areas of your life. Make sure you plan an evening when you are not catching up with housework, or use a Saturday to spend time together away from the routine things. If you create space like that, you will find you are better equipped to tackle the fast pace of life.

*Learn to squeeze extra minutes into a day.* We cannot create extra hours in a day, but we can pick up wasted minutes. By getting up half an hour earlier in the morning or turning the TV off you will be surprised at how you can discover time you thought you did not have.

## Romance is here to stay

Before your wedding you may have taken hours to get ready to meet your fiancé, but now you are living under the same roof there is not the same incentive, let alone the time. But keeping romance alive in a relationship is important. When you prepared to meet him in your courting days the unspoken signal he picked up from all your preparations was that he mattered to you. You wanted to look your best because you wanted to please him. If you now ignore how you look, you are communicating that it no longer matters what your husband thinks.

It is easy to go overboard on this and end up spending hours in the bathroom and a small fortune at The Body Shop. But learning to care how you look is a reflection of how you care for your husband. Romance is important in a growing marriage, and it takes more than sloppy greetings cards to achieve it.

*Looking right.* Try not to lose sight of dressing well and taking time over your appearance. You do not need to have a vast budget to keep your appearance neat and stylish. Be yourself, but take some time in putting yourself together.

The way you look reflects on your husband. Proverbs 31 gives an interesting picture of the ideal wife. One part of it reads, 'She is clothed in fine linen and purple. Her husband is respected at the city gate, where he takes his seat among the elders of the land' (Pr. 31:22–23).

*Learn to communicate.* Some women tend to lapse into moody silences when things are not going well. Or you may find that emotional outbursts are more your way of responding to problems. Part of the process of adjusting to married life is learning how to communicate your feelings to your partner. Learn to talk with your husband. If something is concerning you, find a time to tell him about it. Resorting to the tactics of fallen female nature does not bring out the best in fallen males!

*Don't let 'the curse' be a curse.* Some of us use the menstrual cycle as an excuse for a lot of things. All women, during a major part of their lives, have to come to terms with the monthly period. The difference is that while many carry on with life as normal (with a few limitations) others seem determined that the world should suffer along with them. There are those for whom the monthly period is an excruciatingly painful business. Premenstrual tension (PMT) is recognized by doctors as a medical condition that does cause some women a great deal of difficulty. The good news is that it can be treated. If this is a particular problem then you need to consult your doctor and ask his advice. If you are attending the Family Planning Clinic for contraceptive advice, you will also find help there. Make sure that during those few days each month you are not spreading doom and gloom in your home. Your husband will soon notice how at certain times of the month you experience changes in your emotions as well as your body. If he is mature enough he will respond with sympathy and practical care. Let him help you and resist the temptation of self-pity.

*Accept yourself.* We are amazed at the number of Christian women who are ashamed of how they look. There are reasons for this, we believe, but this is not the place to develop that particular theme. Marriage can be a great means of healing in this respect. It can also work the opposite way if there is little love and kind words are absent. Let your husband love you, and believe him when he compliments you. Learn to accept how you look. The magazines may tell you that your bust is too small or your hips are too big, and you may secretly wish you could afford to have a nose-job done. But God has created you and your husband loves you. Accept yourself and grow as a person with a sense of worth and self-respect.

## Adapting to someone else

Two becoming one takes time. Part of the process of courtship is to help you to get to know your partner and his likes and dislikes. Even after a particularly close courtship you will still discover things you never knew about your husband.

You may well have different ways of doing things, and you will need to adjust to the awful possibility that your husband's way of doing a job is actually better! Your personal lifestyle will have to adapt to that of your partner and *vice versa*.

One of the really enjoyable things about the early years of marriage is this business of adapting to living with another human being. If you keep your sense of humour and are willing to admit you are sometimes wrong, you will survive. And what's more, you'll find it fun!

To use an illustration from our own early years of marriage, we found it quite difficult to adjust to having two very different body-clocks. Ruth is a natural early riser, and within seconds of waking up can be out of bed getting her day organized. But after 10 pm her world used to draw its curtains.

Ian, on the other hand, refused to believe that anyone *could* communicate before 8 am, but at the other end of the day, when everyone else was going to bed, he would be bursting with energy and looking for things to do.

We had to reach a compromise. As the years have gone by we have discovered a pattern that suits us. Basically we both now get up early and we both stay up until the early hours as well! We had to learn to adapt our personal preferences to the other person's needs, something which is always worth doing in a loving relationship.

### Growing together in God

Spiritual growth is part of developing a healthy marriage. We need to maintain a personal walk with God as well as developing together as a couple.

Why do we list growing together in God under adjustments women need to make? Only because through countless conversations we have found that women have more difficulties in this area. For some it is because their partner is a non-Christian. For others, he is a Christian but he may not be expressive about his faith.

Here are a few of the adjustment needs that have come to light. A wife may feel she is 'further on' spiritually than her partner, and may even have been a Christian for a longer period of time. She may find it easier to talk about personal faith than her husband does. She may find it easier to pray out loud or take a lead in studying the Bible. (It is worth mentioning that one reason for this may be experience rather than spirituality. There are more groups geared for women to meet informally to pray and share their faith than there are for men. Women also tend to be more expressive about personal needs than men.)

There are no instant solutions to these situations, particularly if your partner is not a committed Christian. The way to achieve that is through persistent prayer and a lot of loving kindness.

From our own experience, as well as that of our friends who have felt able to share with us freely on these personal areas, there seem to be a few guidelines to follow.

*Don't neglect your own time with God.* Reading the word of God, developing a prayer life and maintaining strong links of fellowship with other Christians are essential ingredients for a balanced diet for the inner life.

*Be patient with your partner.* Guard against criticism and making wrong judgments. There could be reasons of which you are not aware for his apparent lack of interest in spiritual things.

*Talk it through with your partner.* Choose your time and

words carefully, and make constructive suggestions about ways in which you can move forward together.

*Don't be afraid to take a lead.* It needs to be done tactfully and in a non-threatening manner. But instead of sitting there waiting for an initiative that never comes, you should begin to establish regular prayer and sharing times.

*Don't make comparisons.* Some friends of ours have confessed to trying to make their husbands into people God didn't want them to be! Perhaps God does not want your partner to pray like the vicar or preach like Billy Graham, but you are (perhaps subconsciously) trying to make that happen.

We do not want to appear to be playing down the importance of a married couple developing together spiritually. It is just that those who have been through similar experiences have confessed afterwards that being over-zealous, and sometimes downright unrealistic, has not helped the situation greatly. If no progress is made over a period of a few months, or if there is a serious blockage in your communications, then you need to seek advice from your church leaders or a Christian couple that you respect and can trust.

## Love means respect

The New English Bible translates Ephesians 5:33 as: 'The woman must see to it that she pays her husband all respect.' Although the sergeant-major style tone of the translation is not very helpful, the use of the word 'respect' is worth noting.

If you love your partner then you will respect him. It is sad to see a couple who have lost respect for each other and, perhaps by using humour and ridicule, tear each other apart in front of others.

1 Corinthians 13 is a passage in the Bible that is well worth memorizing. Interestingly, it is one of the most popular Bible readings chosen for a wedding service. The love it speaks of applies to every human relationship, but it helps us to understand what the word 'respect' should mean within a

marriage partnership. Read it for yourself:

> Love is kind and patient,
> Never jealous, boastful, proud or rude.
> Love isn't selfish or quick-tempered.
> It doesn't keep a record of wrongs that others do.
> Love rejoices in the truth, but not in evil.
> Love is always supportive, loyal, hopeful, and trusting.
> Love never fails!
>
> (1 Cor. 13:4–8, Contemporary English Version)

## Giving and taking

It seems that another important adjustment women find they need to make concerns money and the whole matter of learning to share. You may have smiled inwardly at the part of the wedding service which says 'for richer, for poorer', as you probably consider that wealth will not be a major problem! However much or little God entrusts to you, it is just that: a trust, a responsibility from him.

As a single woman you have probably enjoyed a certain amount of financial independence. Now with joint responsibilities you will discover that spending habits have to change. Later on, as and when you decide to stop work and start a family, you will make another surrender of independence, at least for a few years.

Acceptance is easy to preach but difficult to practise. But as a wife you need to accept that a certain loss of independence has come and will come. We strongly advise joint financial arrangements in marriage, and later, when we deal with money management in more detail, we shall explain how important it is to ensure true equality between partners in such matters.

A husband and wife *both* need to develop the skill of managing joint finances. But a significantly large proportion of newly-wed wives admit that this sense of losing their financial independence is something they need to work through.

The way to adjust to these new circumstances is to make sure that your attitude is right. We like Tim La Haye's punchy comment: 'Marriage is a joint venture between two people who live as one. It is not two distinct corporations doing business under the same roof.'[1]

Learning to share is a mutual responsibility, but if you are a woman, be prepared to keep a 'giving' attitude as you set out on your joint partnership.

Having looked at some of the individual adjustments we need to make as a wife or a husband, here are some of the changes we will need to face together.

## Adjusting to life together

Married couples can, if they are not careful, become selfish, insular people. As leaders in a local church we are used to hearing the cry from single friends: 'Since those two got married, they haven't got time for anyone else!' We need to hear that criticism and learn not to shut ourselves off, particularly from those who have been good friends in the past.

In adjusting to married life you will need to strike a number of careful balances. Time together is important, especially in the early months of married life. But so is time with friends and one of the best ways to avoid shutting yourself away is to get into the hospitality habit.

If God has given you a home, then start to use it. It doesn't matter if it is a mansion or a bedsit, you can use it to bless others. There is no need to confine your invitations to your own circle of friends; look around your local congregation and you will discover a ready-made guest list of all ages, shapes and sizes. There are elderly people who live alone, single parents who rarely have a night out, and couples with small families who could do with a break. Hospitality may seem small and insignificant, but in fact it is one of the most important and overlooked spiritual gifts in a local church.

As you enjoy the early years of adjusting to life as a married couple, fight hard to keep your relationship open to others and not simply a selfish affair. We can achieve this by remembering that:

- we are not meant to be self-sufficient
- God has given us a home for others to benefit from as well
- we are made richer through relationships with others
- hospitality is a neglected spiritual gift
- single people want to retain our friendship
- contact with non-Christians through hospitality is vital

The temptation facing any newly-weds is to become an island, but God wants you to become a bridge. Most people recognize that you need time together to build your home and relationship. But make a determined commitment that you will not cut yourselves off in isolation from relationships where you can give and receive so much.

## Adjusting to the wider family

When we were planning to write this book we had no intention of including this particular section. But after listening to Christian couples who talked freely with us about their own experiences, we felt it was a subject that we could not afford to ignore. It is really a joint adjustment that a husband and wife need to be willing to make. It is all to do with learning to be part of a wider family.

You chose to marry each other, and (we hope!) you are glad about that decision. But along with your partner you have inherited his or her parents, grandparents – a whole army of relatives as well. You will have to learn to develop and maintain a relationship with them, however difficult it may be.

As with all human relationships, you need to work at building links between yourselves as a couple and your in-laws. Here are some positive steps that you can take in this direction.

*Be loyal to each other.* Resist the temptation to moan to your parents about your partner. This can create tension and insecurity.

*Maintain your independence.* As a married couple you have to make your own mistakes, and learn from them. Parents can advise and support you, but in your new relationship you both need to make your own decisions. There is a thin line between advice and interference, and although the former is often welcome from parents, the latter should be resisted at all costs. Perhaps one set of parents do not get on particularly well with their opposite numbers, and this in turn creates tension between you as a couple. Refuse to become pawns in anyone else's game. Be scrupulously fair in the time you spend with each other's parents and treat both sets with respect, refusing to get drawn into commenting about the other side of the family. It is the best way to maintain a Christian testimony and will help to pull down a few barricades that may have been built up.

*Care for your parents.* For some couples marriage can mean severing links with our families in a way that God never intended. One of the Ten Commandments is that we should honour parents (Ex. 20:12). That debt of honour, respect, love and practical care continues as long as they are alive. Your parents may not be Christians, they may not have always treated you in a way that you would agree with, but, for better or worse, they remain your parents who deserve your love.

Have you ever thanked your parents for all that they have done for you over the years? If you find it hard to say face to face, write a letter, send a card or a bouquet of flowers. Let them know that you love and appreciate them. The importance of expressing thanks will become clear to you when you become parents yourselves.

*Face problems, don't bury them.* You do not have to dig too deep in many families to discover people who have stopped talking to each other. Perhaps the incident that built a wall of silence was quite small in proportion to the problems it has caused. Sooner or later tensions will arise that can, if they are not dealt with quickly, begin to affect you as a married couple.

We have learned that the only way to handle tensions within the wider family is to bring them into the open. A word of caution, though. Not *every* little incident is worth raising after the event. We are talking about the sort of difficulties, jealousies and relationship problems that every family faces from time to time where the issues become big enough to divide us. Honesty is the best policy, and if you can agree together on a course of action, pray it through, then gently face the issue with those concerned.

Every marriage is unique. This is because the two people who make up the relationship are unique human beings. We bring into the partnership our different backgrounds and experiences of life. We blend these with our individual personalities and mix them in with the personal circumstances that surround us in the first years of married life. But for all the differences that exist, the principles of adjustment remain the same.

Adjusting to each other within marriage takes time, so don't feel you are complete failures if, in the first few years, some of the things we have discussed in this chapter crop up in your own lives. There is also the pressure of comparing our marriage with another couple's, and feeling inferior because the difficulties you are both wrestling with never seem to bother them. God may be taking you a different way, teaching you different lessons because he wants to do different things with you. Your marriage is unique, and provided that you face up to the adjustments you need to make with patience, honesty, a sense of humour and total dependence on God, you will make it. Believe us, it is well worth the effort.

## Second time around

In a chapter dealing with some of the adjustments couples face, it is worth adding some thoughts for those who are setting out on marriage for the second time.

It may be that one of you has been married before (or you both have). If this is the case, you will be bringing previous marital experiences into your new relationship. Some of these will inevitably be bad experiences, but we hope there will be good ones as well.

It is impossible in the short space of a few lines to cover all the issues that are likely to be involved if you are setting out on a second marriage relationship. But we can summarize some of the adjustments you are likely to face.

## Deal with the past

The breakdown of a marriage is a painful experience for everyone involved. No-one walks away without scars. In your own divorce you can probably list a number of people who have been hurt, yourself included.

As far as it depends on you, the past needs to be dealt with. If you are a committed Christian, you will know what the Bible says about forgiveness and putting things right. You cannot turn the clock back and undo things, but you can stop them affecting you today and in the future.

We have known examples of people writing to their former partners, long after a divorce has gone through, to express repentance or forgiveness. They have done this out of a desire to deal with the past in a positive way.

Some of us bury past mistakes, believing that any attempt to go over them will be too painful. In fact, the opposite is true. When we face the past honestly, we find healing when we let go of negative feelings such as anger, hatred and the desire for revenge.

You may require skilled help in working some of these things through, and if this is the case we suggest you begin by approaching a leader in your local church. It is best to tackle this before your wedding if at all possible.

## Learning from mistakes

One of the first questions we ask someone who is marrying for a second time is: 'What have you learned from your previous marriage that you are bringing into this one?' There may be good experiences you look back on with joy, as well as mistakes you would rather not repeat. The important thing is to build on what you have learned, through both types of experience.

Don't keep these lessons to yourself; share with your partner the things you want to tackle as you learn from the past. But be careful to avoid constantly referring back to your previous relationship in a way that makes your partner feel threatened.

George made that mistake. Having been married for forty years, his wife died with cancer. He married a woman called Beryl, who had been a good family friend for many years. Beryl, who had never been married before, felt that she was an absolute beginner, although she was in her late fifties. She felt unable to match up to George's wife's standards in any department of the marriage. What made matters worse were George's constant references to his previous marriage. He had no intention of making Beryl feel inadequate (although that was the result). The truth was that he was still going through the grieving process. He missed his first wife greatly, and part of his way of handling this was constantly to bring her name into the conversation. Things came to a head one summer when George insisted, for the third year running, that they return to the same holiday location that he and his first wife had visited every summer. Beryl seized the opportunity for a long-overdue talk about the past, and their future.

It was a turning-point for them both. But George had to

accept the need to let go of his previous marriage, without in any way letting go of the wonderful memories and links with his first wife. Beryl had some learning to do as well about dealing with her insecurities and accepting that George loved her for who she was, and not as a pale substitute for his first wife.

## Work on your relationships

From conversations with friends who are in second-time marriages, they identify family relationships as a major area of adjustment. Perhaps there are children from your first marriage and you have either custody of them or access to them.

In your new marriage, there may be children from your partner's previous marriage to whom you become a step-parent. This means that there will be regular contact with a collection of people including former marriage partners, other family members, former friends and the like. It is inevitable that tensions will arise from time to time.

It is important to prepare yourselves for the complexities involved and determine to do all you can, by God's grace, to keep relationships happy and smooth. We realize that it is easier said than done, but neglect in this area puts pressure on your new relationship.

A friend recently confided that her husband's former wife insisted on ringing at regular intervals to discuss a range of matters relating to maintenance and access to the children. She noticed that her husband was always affected by these telephone calls, both physically and emotionally. They could ruin an evening or a weekend and create tensions between them. In the end they decided on a better way of dealing with such arrangements that took it out of the home. They did so in a way that attempted to keep good relationships all round. This was all the more important since the husband had become a Christian since the breakup of his first marriage.

## Should we get married in church?

This is a question that couples involved in a second-time-around relationship usually ask. You need to check with your local church on their policy about marrying divorced people. In some denominations this is not allowed, although they sometimes will suggest a service of blessing following a registry-office wedding. Other churches will accept the possibility of conducting a church service where one or both of the partners is divorced, but the minister will want to be satisfied about your reasons for requesting to be married in church.

We have been in the position many times of talking to couples wanting to be remarried in church. One of the main things we look for at such times is a *genuine acknowledgment of failure in the past and a desire to seek God's help for the future*. The Bible talks about repentance: a change of mind which leads to a change of direction.

Divorce is not God's ideal, but in a world filled with fallen people it is one sad, inevitable result of sin. With an acknowledgment of our own failure and a willingness to build towards something better, with God's help we can move forward.

## Notes

[1] Tim La Haye, *How to Stay Happy Though Married* (Tyndale House Publishers), p. 79.

# CHAPTER FOUR

# WE DON'T
## TALK ANY MORE

John and Anne set out on married life believing that their happiness was 'written in the stars'. Two years further on, the stars had begun to fall from the sky. They shared their disappointments with a national newspaper in a feature article on divorce. Their sad story provides an example of how communication breakdown in marriage can have serious consequences.

'I couldn't believe it,' says John, who works for a major computer company. 'No two people could have been more in love than we were. Then we married, and woosh! The whole thing is draining away faster than water through a colander. I have this very difficult job, very stressful, what with takeovers, redundancies and the new technology. And when I get home at night I like to relax. You know, watch a bit of telly, have a glass of wine, unwind. But all she wants to do is discuss things like new curtains, and when I'm going to cut the grass, and why I haven't said I love her fifty times a day. "When, when, why, why?" It's driving me crazy.'

Anne gives her view of the problems: 'I thought that marriage was a partnership. I want to share. All he wants is a live-in housekeeper who is seen but never heard. He thinks more of his dog.'

In this chapter we are looking at how we can learn to communicate effectively with each other within marriage. John and Anne found that after two years they had drifted apart. Good communication would have helped them to grow closer together.

'Relate' is an organization dedicated to helping people get along together. They have recognized the importance of couples learning to talk to each other. One of their staff even suggested including another vow in the wedding service in which couples would promise to talk! She continued, 'If only couples would or could communicate more it would make a tremendous difference.' One piece of research has indicated that in a twenty-four-hour period, the average couple spend around twelve minutes in real conversation with each other. That is hardly the way to build a strong relationship!

## Communication is a key

Communication is a key that unlocks many different doors in your relationship. If you want to grow together in your relationship with God, or develop a fulfilling and healthy sex life, or learn to manage money properly, good communication is the key.

We sometimes fall into the trap of thinking that communication means 'telling my husband or wife exactly what I think'. But good communication involves *listening* as much as *telling*. It is not a rifle range where opinions are shot at a lifeless target, but more like a tennis match where words are exchanged like a ball between two players. In his helpful book *Look Who's Talking*, Peter Cotterell explains the five stages involved in human communication:

- *conception:* thinking out a message
- *encoding:* deciding how to send the message
- *transmission:* sending the message
- *reception:* receiving the message, hearing it; and perhaps
- *perception:* understanding the message.[1]

Without getting too technical, it is obvious that there is quite a gap between *conception* (thinking out what I want to say) and *perception* (my partner understanding what I'm saying).

When you add in human factors such as tiredness, pressure of work and the emotional ups and downs we all face, it is perhaps easier to understand how arguments occur.

Learning to communicate well with each other involves being willing to share the real 'me', and to listen to my partner opening up about himself or herself. It may start with peripheral things such as personal tastes in clothes, the daily routine and our jobs. It needs to move to the deeper areas of our hearts as we learn to express our dreams, fears and hopes.

## Learning to communicate

Developing the skill of good communication is a continual process. We have tried to look honestly at our own marriage in writing this chapter, and we have realized how problems can often be resolved when we are willing to give time to talking things through. We share some ways in which we have learned, and are still learning, about keeping the lines of communication open.

### Be involved in each other's lives

You probably have jobs in separate places, making it impossible to share every working minute together. That is not a bad thing! But at the end of the day it is good to develop the habit of talking over what has been happening. Show an interest in what your partner is doing. You may not understand the technicalities of the job but you can enter into part of it. Tact and understanding are needed here. Our personalities differ, and it could be that at the end of a long, hard day you need time to unwind and find yourself again. John and Anne, who told their story to a national newspaper, needed to learn about giving and taking. Anne could have given John more space when he came home exhausted, and he should have recognized her need of companionship at the end of a lonely day. Sadly, they found it easier to be more open with a journalist than they had ever been with each other.

It boils down to thinking about your partner's needs. This skill is developed through learning to 'read' the other person's signals, and giving ourselves to each other.

Something that may help you here is to make a general rule to treat the first half hour when you arrive home as a special event. You can then use these thirty minutes as a time to talk over some of the things that have happened to you both during the day. After this you can begin to relax and unwind. It sounds simple, but some couples actually find that simply adopting this mental attitude helps them to be more considerate of their partner's needs.

## Treat your partner as
## the most important person in your life

Jesus once said, 'For where your treasure is, there your heart will be also' (Mt. 6:21). What matters to us most will occupy our greatest attention. Treat each other as important, and this will automatically affect your desire to communicate your innermost thoughts to your partner. It is very easy to take each other for granted and become careless in our everyday conversations.

If you treat your husband or wife as important it will help you to get your priorities in order. Build a strong friendship together in the early years, particularly before you decide to start a family. When children arrive, time together is more difficult to find, so develop good communication habits early in your marriage.

## Learn to listen

Most of us find listening more difficult than talking. As someone once pointed out, God gave us two ears and one mouth, which may indicate that we should listen twice as much as we talk. One way to avoid an argument is to listen hard to what your partner is saying. Don't just react to criticism but try to discover the truth that is probably contained within it. As human beings we tend to bottle things up inside ourselves and, if they are not given proper release, they can lead to outbursts of temper, tears and, on occasions, physical violence. A safety-valve for those tensions is to share knowing that someone is really listening to you. There may be times when you simply need to let your husband or wife pour out those bottled-up feelings. You may not have instant answers to the problems, but the fact you are listening to him or her shows you care.

### Be open

Openness takes time to develop and it also takes trust. Before you share your deepest thoughts with another person you need to be assured of that person's love and commitment to you.

When we were first married we believed we were open with each other. But as our relationship grew, we found ourselves learning to share things in our lives that we had previously not admitted even to ourselves. Make a pledge to each other to work on building an open relationship in which you can develop an atmosphere of trust.

We once met a couple who told us about some of the problems they had faced in their first few years of married life. They had found it hard to talk together and had experienced real difficulties in the sexual side of their relationship. The wife confessed to having violent outbursts of temper which were often sparked off by trivial incidents. They told how the wife, as a small child, had been the victim of a serious sexual assault which had never come to light. She had tried to bury this unpleasant incident but her memory kept it very much alive. Filled with guilt, shame and pain she had limped into marriage determined to keep her past a secret. One day, at bursting-point, the whole messy story had flooded out, and through a loving husband and skilful counselling, the love of God cleaned out the past and filled her with new hope.

Openness had released the floodgates. We urged them, as we urge you, not to forget to keep practising openness

## It's not what you say,
### it's the way that you say it

Most of us wish, at some time or another, that we had the ability of tape recorders to erase a clumsy sentence and record over it again. Unfortunately, hasty words cannot be taken back. And words can hurt us badly.

Be on your guard against saying the right thing in the wrong way. The best rule we know is 'Think before you speak'. It is staggering how many arguments develop from a careless word. No wonder the Bible describes our small tongues as 'a restless evil, full of deadly poison' (Jas. 3:8).

There is a need to be particularly aware of this when you are both tired. It is easy for molehills to turn into mountains late at night! We have found that it is sometimes advisable to leave discussing an issue until after a good night's sleep, when you can both face things in a better frame of mind.

## Don't duck issues; face them

Two free-minded individuals are bound to have strong disagreements at times. Building a strong marriage as a Christian couple does *not* consist of meekly saying 'Yes, dear' whenever conflicts arise. Our backgrounds shape our opinions. Experiences of the past influence today's decisions. Because of these factors there will be times when even the closest couple will find their attitudes conflict. It may be something as 'small' as choosing the colour of the new living-room curtains, but differences of opinion are bound to occur. If we learn to face these differences with maturity we can grow in our love and understanding of one another. In bringing things into the open we actually help each other to grow.

Burying them solves nothing at all. Selwyn Hughes quotes an anonymous writer:

Take a man and a woman
From totally different homes
With different upbringing and experiences
Each with emotional uniqueness
With different likes and dislikes
Each with some degree of independence
And with some self-centredness
Living in the same house
With different tasks and responsibilities
Working from the same household budget
Trying to meet the same goals. Will they agree on everything?
No way.[2]

We hope you feel as encouraged as we do in realizing that conflicts do not necessarily weaken a marriage. If they are dealt with in the right way, they can actually make your relationship stronger.

### Learn to say sorry

Back in the 1970s the box-office blockbuster movie, *Love Story*, carried the subtitle, 'Love means never having to say you're sorry.' This just goes to show how little Hollywood understands about real life! Also from the other side of the Atlantic, but filled with more common sense, Cliff Barrows, of the Billy Graham team, has written about the three most important phrases for a husband and wife: 'I love you'; 'I am sorry'; 'Please forgive me.'

To admit that you are wrong is a tough experience. Some of us would prefer to let the incident be quickly forgotten. But God lays down a biblical pattern for forgiveness. We need to admit we are wrong, be prepared to turn from doing wrong and, where appropriate, to put things right. Always practise saying sorry.

## Coping with conflicts

One modern version of the wedding service includes this promise: 'I will love you in good times and bad. I will love you when it is easy and love you when it is difficult …' It is a useful reminder that, for all the joys of married life, there are difficulties to be faced as well.

You may feel that this is a pessimistic view. We believe it is realistic to face the fact that difficulties will come, but equally to believe they can be overcome with God's help.

We had been married only a few months when we were visiting a church for a weekend. We were invited to the home of an elderly lady for a meal. We were deeply impressed by this godly woman who told us of her husband who had died a few years previously. She remembered him with deep affection and he was obviously a Christian whose life had influenced many others. She looked back over fifty years of marriage and delivered the devastating comment, 'My dears, in all those years I can never remember us having a cross word or a single disagreement.' The words hit home hard.

Weeks later – in the middle of a heated argument – her words came back to us. We both admitted feeling terrible failures in the light of such a shining example. To us it seemed as though a week never went by without us falling out over something. Feeling very condemned, we decided to try to salvage our 'wreck of a marriage'. Looking back, we now appreciate that we were simply going through the process of adjustment. We also now realize that the lady whose words had challenged us was idealizing her late husband, something that bereaved people often do as part of their grief. She was not being dishonest, but simply remembering the good times that she had experienced in her marriage and subconsciously choosing to forget the difficulties she had once faced.

We share that incident here as it may prevent you from feeling condemned when you compare yourselves with another couple who look as though they never exchange a cross word. No two marriages are identical. Some of our friends react to conflicts with frosty silence, others with heated words. Both responses are natural (that is, they come from our fallen human nature), and both reveal the need for us to 'grow up' in learning to love.

What causes conflicts and the breakdown in communication that often follows? The causes are as varied as the people behind them, but here are some of the main ones.

### Different personalities

In your marriage one of you may be quiet, reflective and more of an introvert, whereas the other partner is impulsive and extrovert in personality. Because of these differences, our reactions to a given situation are not the same. One partner may be rock-solid when a really big crisis comes and yet fall apart over the most trivial problems. One of you may be more subject to moods, leaving you on top of the world on Tuesday and in the depths of despair by Wednesday lunchtime. Learning to understand how you and your partner tick as people will help you learn to communicate better when conflicts occur.

### An unhealed past

We all pick up emotional scars during our lives, some of which can have a serious effect on our close relationships. But the good news is that, by his death on the cross and through his powerful resurrection, Jesus Christ has made salvation possible. The root meaning of the word 'salvation' is wholeness. We can be made whole people through the work that Jesus has completed. 'He himself bore our sins in his body on the tree [cross] so that we might die to sins and live for righteousness; by his wounds you have been healed' (1 Pet. 2:24).

For some of us, this wholeness comes as we grow in our

Christian faith. Our insecurities and emotional scars are dealt with gradually as we open our lives to the power of God's Spirit. Others need the help of Christians who understand these things. Often they are people who have experienced God's healing work in their own lives. None of us needs to live as prisoners of the past. Jesus said, 'If the Son sets you free, you will be free indeed' (Jn. 8:36).

You may be aware that your reactions have a root deep in the past. The first step to discovering freedom comes when you share that in honesty with your partner, and then together you can face it with God.

Perhaps you are afraid of your partner's reaction if you opened up about the past. That is a risk, we admit, but if your partner truly loves you, it is a risk worth taking.

## Christian growth

Conflicts arise between couples because one partner (or both) has not yet grown up enough. With our own children we have gone through stages where one of them will throw down a toy, burst into tears and run out of the room. You can cope with that in a seven-year-old, but when people are doing that at the age of twenty-seven it is evidence of a lack of maturity. We recognize that in our own early years of marriage, some of the arguments boiled down to basic immaturity. God had to deal with pride, temper, selfishness, jealousy and a whole list of other things. That is not to say that we have now arrived. The old nature needs putting to death every day of our lives (see Col. 3:5ff.).

In your own Christian life, identify where growth is needed. Invite God to take control of your attitudes and reactions. Learn to grow as a mature man or woman of faith.

## Tough circumstances

Pressures through outside circumstances can cause conflicts within a marriage. Christian couples we have talked with pinpointed worries about money, demanding jobs, bad living accommodation, health problems and tensions in the wider family as causes of arguments. In some of these situations we have no power to change things, which adds to the feeling of frustration.

It is a human tendency, when things go wrong, to look for someone to shoulder the blame. Our marriage partner can be an easy target for this. 'United we stand, divided we fall' is the principle to follow. However tough the circumstances, we need to face them together. This is where the commitment of love needs to be demonstrated. Isolating yourself will not make the circumstances vanish, but standing together you will discover strength in each other.

## Spiritual warfare

It is all too easy to blame the devil for everything that goes wrong in our lives. Sometimes it is our own stupidity that leads to conflict. But at the same time, we are told in the New Testament that we have an enemy who 'prowls around like a roaring lion looking for someone to devour' (1 Pet. 5:8).

You may have noticed that conflicts often occur at important times in your spiritual life. It took us some time to realize that Sunday was often the day when tensions would arise. There is only one thing worse than arriving late at church still fuming over an argument at the breakfast table, and that is to attempt to lead a congregation in worship when you are boiling on the inside and out of fellowship with your partner.

The Scripture gives us sound advice on dealing with the devil: 'Resist him, standing firm in the faith' (1 Pet. 5:9). Recognize that you are in a spiritual battle. Prepare for those attacks by prayer and being alert. Any Christian couple determined for God's best in their lives are going to be targets for the enemy, so learn early on to use the armour and the weapons given to make us winners.

## Resolving conflict

We were tempted to call this part of the chapter 'How to have a good argument', but thought better of it! But there are ways to have a *good* argument. Take Paul's advice to the Ephesian Christians as an example: 'If you become angry, do not let your anger lead you into sin, and do not stay angry all day. Don't give the Devil a chance' (Eph. 4:26–27, GNB).

How do we learn to express anger without being led into sin? Here are two examples of how *not* to do it.

Graham admits that he talks first and thinks later. In his marriage he always speaks his mind and believes in 'putting his wife straight' whether they are alone or in company. He believes he is rarely (if ever) wrong on any issue, and even if he is, 'sorry' is just not part of his vocabulary. When it comes to a disagreement, Graham does most of the talking, although it is mainly shouting. His easy command of language and selective memory mean he can develop a powerful case to prove himself right in every subject from whether his tea was served late to why they are overdrawn at the bank. The situation is resolved by Graham's wife always taking the initiative in apologizing. Things gradually return to normal, until the next time.

Karen learned everything she knows about marriage from her father, who patiently put up with her overpowering mother for forty years of hard married labour. Karen is determined never to be as bossy or opinionated as her mother. Dad's way of dealing with things had been to retreat to the garden, take the dog for a walk or watch cricket in the park. As a busy mum, Karen has few such escape routes. Instead she has learned how to hide within herself. She never expresses her true feelings and feels physically sick when any arguments occur with her husband. He expresses his anger, while she just freezes inside and says nothing. Karen has now developed the ability to run away from everything. She is happy for her husband to make the decisions he wants to make and she organizes her world in her own way. Karen has stopped listening, because it causes too much pain. 'A happy life is a quiet life' is her motto, so she avoids conflicts by saying nothing and ignoring the issues. Things always get back to normal, until the next time.

You will not be surprised to learn that neither Graham nor Karen is building a strong marriage. Every day of their lives they are sowing more seeds of self-destruction, and, unless some outside help is received, they are heading for disaster. Is there any practical help for them, and for us, in learning how to disagree? We pass on some lessons we are still learning.

### Find the right time

It is a good rule never to argue in front of other people. Like all rules, it gets broken occasionally, but it is worth maintaining. Certain times of the day (such as last thing at night, or when you are about to leave for work) put pressures on you that lead to hasty reactions. We do not live in an ideal world, and we are not suggesting that marital disagreements can be planned like summer holidays. We have discovered that we both have a filing tray in our memories marked 'Pending'. We can come back to things later when there is more time and, all being well, less heat.

It takes enormous self-discipline to do this, particularly if your emotions feel like a boiling kettle, but learn to find the right time to express your feelings.

### Choose your words

Unkind words cut deep. Be sensitive how you express yourself. Dragging up past incidents and making cruel personal comments do nothing to help your case or build up your partner. It is possible to win an argument and lose a friend, so choose your words with care.

Graham (whom we mentioned earlier) cannot understand

why his wife is unresponsive to his love-making. When he is in bed, he has forgotten his tirade of words at the dinner table. But his wife still hurts deeply. Words can be more brutal than fists, and it is hard to express passion when you feel battered.

## Express your feelings

It is wrong to hide your feelings on the assumption that this is the Christian thing to do. If you want to develop an open relationship, then learn to talk about your feelings of anger. Karen is sentencing herself to the same miserable marriage that her parents endured. She has to break the sound barrier and stop hiding her feelings.

## Hear your partner out

Have you found yourself in a situation where, having poured out your frustration, you take a break while your partner replies? What are you doing in those moments? Catching your breath, marshalling your next few points or building up a head of steam for round 2? Try listening. Hear what your husband or wife is saying. You may even learn something!

## Pray

Some issues cannot be sorted out in a few minutes. Perhaps your disagreement is a deep matter. If, in a time of conflict, you can learn to pray together, you are practising God's pattern for marriage, which is designed as a trio, not a duet.

We have prayed, at times, when we have been out of fellowship with each other. It is tempting to carry on the argument in prayer with high-sounding phrases, but that is not effective praying. When we come together before God we are bringing our lives under the authority of the external reference point we all need. Prayer can turn to tears, and even laughter. It provides perspective on the problem and brings peace into disturbed lives. You do not have to feel 'holy' before you pray, just dependent and willing for God to change you. We have often come away from a time of prayer feeling forgiven, closer together and a few steps nearer to finding a solution to our original disagreement.

### Forgive and forget

God's forgiveness is so rich and full it is indescribable. The psalmist says, 'As far as the east is from the west, so far has he removed our transgressions from us' (Ps. 103:12). Too often we become caught up in the wonder of such forgiveness and ignore its implications. Jesus answered Peter's question about how many times he should forgive his brother with the stark reply, 'I tell you, not seven times, but seventy-seven times' (Mt. 18:22).

If we confess our sins to God they are covered (see 1 Jn. 1:9). If we have asked forgiveness of each other then it is wrong to try to uncover what is past. For most of us forgiveness is one issue, but learning to forget is a more difficult business. If we can put past mistakes behind us, having learned by them, we will prevent bitterness gaining a stranglehold on our hearts.

### SOS

If you have ever spent hours trying to find out why your car will not start, you may have experienced the sense of relief when a qualified mechanic arrives and makes sense of all those parts you have taken off the engine and can't fit back on again. There is nothing wrong in asking for help. Admitting our need of help is something which we do not need to be ashamed of. There are times within most marriages when help from the outside is much appreciated. This may come about informally, through another couple perhaps, who come alongside us just when we need to talk things over with someone. More formal ways of finding help are through leaders in our local church or Christians who specialize in helping married couples. An approach to your family doctor or staff at the Family Planning Clinic is one way of receiving expert help, and secular organizations such as Relate exist to give advice to couples. (There are some useful addresses listed at the back of this book.) Whatever your needs, you are not the first couple who have had to face them. Other people have worked things out and, with God's help, you can as well. Ignoring the problems will not make them go away, of that you can be certain.

Just before our wedding a friend gave us some timely advice about the most important thing to pack and take on our honeymoon. We waited with bated breath as he made the great revelation: 'A sense of humour!' We packed it and have tried to take it with us ever since. The Bible says, 'A cheerful heart is good medicine, but a crushed spirit dries up the bones' (Pr. 17:22). Conflicts can be avoided, made easier to handle and brought more quickly to an end through a balanced sense of humour. If you can laugh at yourself you will be a nicer person to live with.

## An oasis in the desert

We began this chapter with John and Anne who, after two years of married life, found themselves drifting apart. They both admitted that real communication was just not happening between them. Probably one of their worst enemies is yours too. Time (or, to be precise, lack of time) is one of the biggest blockages to good communication.

If you both have demanding jobs and a desire to be active members of a local church, time together is going to be limited. But what you lack in *quantity* of time together you can make up for in the *quality* of the time you share.

In the nation of Israel a policy was followed which came directly from the law of God: 'If a man has recently married, he must not be sent to war or have any other duty laid on him. For one year he is to be free to stay at home and bring happiness to the wife he has married' (Dt. 24:5).

God recognizes the need for us to take time to build a strong friendship, to grow in our understanding and enjoyment of each other and to lay a strong foundation for the future. Without becoming exclusive you need to learn how to guard your times together.

We have discovered how to create an oasis at regular intervals. An oasis is a place of refreshment in a desert. It is a place to rest, be fed and watered. It is a place to be renewed. In the busy pace of life, days, weeks or even months slip by without our finding time to spend together and being still enough to share our deep thoughts.

Plan ahead for a regular evening when you can be uninterrupted. Turn the TV off and spend a leisurely meal together talking and listening. Recently, we sat in a wine bar and watched a young couple obviously very much in love. They looked as if they were spending a final few minutes together before separating to go their different ways. The place was packed with people, but they were utterly oblivious of anyone else. We found ourselves moved by their intimacy in the midst of noise. We realized that that is what we constantly have to struggle to achieve: intimacy in the middle of a frantic world.

As well as a regular evening together, take regular opportunities to go out alone. It may be a walk in the park, or window-shopping in the high street. The aim is to go out together without actually having to do anything. Try to plan a weekend away or, if money is short, a special day out. These times can be an oasis for two important reasons.

First, they give you something to aim at. When life seems busy and there is not time to talk through a problem, you can keep going in the knowledge that you have an oasis planned within the next week or so when you will be uninterrupted. Just knowing that fact can release some of the pressure.

Second, an oasis creates the space that is needed for good communication to take place. A relaxing meal or a walk together provides the setting for important things to be discussed without being up against the demands of the clock.

Of course, there is always the danger of creating a false atmosphere. One couple told us, with laughter, how they decided to have an 'evening of communication' and sat there looking at each other in an uncomfortable silence, desperately thinking of something very serious to say. Thankfully they gave up trying and began to relax together.

Create a regular oasis in your marriage. A private place is not, in itself, a selfish thing, but can help you to build the sort of relationship that will refresh others as well.

## Notes

[1]Peter Cotterell, *Look Who's Talking* (Kingsway), p. 37.
[2]Selwyn Hughes, *Marriage as God Intended* (Kingsway), p. 71.

# CHAPTER FIVE

# PARTNERS WITH GOD

On our wedding day we received many cards and letters of
congratulation. But among all the good wishes and helpful
advice that people sent, one verse from the New Testament
stands out in our memories: 'Jesus himself drew near and
went with them' (Lk. 24:15, RSV). It was for us a reminder and
a challenge. It reminded us that God himself had brought us
together in marriage; he was the originator of the relationship.
It was a challenge, too, that we should keep walking with
Jesus, both as individuals and as a couple, if we wanted to
experience God's best in our lives.

The spiritual pillar is an important part of a Christian
marriage. In this chapter we shall take a look at some of the
ways in which a couple can grow together spiritually. We want
to touch on five areas that together help towards spiritual
fitness in marriage.

## Personal growth

When a man and woman are married they become, theo-
logically speaking, 'one flesh'. As they consummate their love
in the act of sexual intercourse, it becomes a physical reality
as well. But at the same time as being 'one flesh', we retain
our individual personalities. We need to grow as individuals as
well as developing together as a couple.

This is particularly true in the realm of spiritual growth.
Praying together should not replace prayer to God by
ourselves. Although we can draw spiritual resources from our

partner, we still need to maintain a close personal walk with God.

One of the demands placed on a newly married couple is that of time. Responsibilities of a new home, demanding jobs and settling into a new routine can combine to make life a constant whirr of activity. Many couples find that the new routine shuts out opportunities to be alone with God for prayer and study of the Bible. We cannot emphasize strongly enough how important it is to develop our individual Christian lives, not to the exclusion of our partner, but with the single-mindedness of those whose hearts are set on knowing God better.

This lesson has come home to us because we have spent many months apart from each other during the course of our marriage. Both of us freely admit that we find the discipline of making time to be alone with God a constant battle. However, it remains worth the struggle, because when we set aside other things to put God at the centre of our lives we find ourselves connecting up to the power-source of life. If your spiritual growth is bound up totally with your partner, or if you constantly look to him or her alone for spiritual leadership, you end up with a lopsided relationship. All the spiritual initiative is focused on one partner instead of being shared equally between the two.

We have discovered (often the hard way) that a close personal walk with God is often a means of encouraging and helping our partner through difficult times. Perhaps one of us has been going through a rough patch, feeling despondent and spiritually dried up, and it has been refreshing to receive support from the other at times like this.

In practical terms, this means maintaining regular times alone with God to read the Scriptures and pray. It also means facing the challenges that God lays on us as individuals to exercise faith and grow in our commitment as disciples of Jesus.

## Prayer and the Word of God

You have probably heard the oft-repeated cliché: 'The couple that prays together stays together.' There's a large element of truth in it, although anyone who sees prayer as a type of lucky charm is in for a shock. It is no use praying unless we are also willing to obey God's principles for successful marriage as well.

There is probably no better way to involve God in the centre of your marriage than by spending time together with him. Most Christian couples accept this as an ideal, but when it comes to working it out in practice they meet all sorts of problems. Two good friends of ours, Mike and Katey Morris, have written a helpful book on the subject entitled *Praying Together*.[1] It is an honest book which we found useful in our own relationship, not least because it sets out so many ways in which a couple can actually learn *how* to develop together spiritually. We want to include a quotation that reveals how much God is wanting to help us grow in prayer:

> He fully appreciates the problems we humans have with prayer. He does not expect you to pledge yourself to a three-hour vigil every night. He understands when having promised faithfully to pray for sick Aunt Mathilda you forget to do so until reminded by a phone call thanking you for your prayers. God created us human, he therefore fully appreciates the nature of our humanity. He is intimately interested in our praying, he is fully committed to guiding us in the 'how to' of prayer, and he totally appreciates the problems we have and the mistakes we make and the failures we experience. But as you'd expect, he urges us to keep going and discover the development we can make. God is on our side rooting for us, so let's get on with it.[2]

The best time to begin to pray together is when you are preparing for marriage. If you are reading this book as an engaged couple we urge you to get into the habit of regularly spending time praying over your future plans together. It is great to start married life having developed the practice of praying through different decisions that you face.

You may have become Christians since your marriage, in which case you need to learn quickly the joy of building up the spiritual side of your relationship. We do not presume to lay down rules, not least because prayer is a very personal exercise of devotion. But we recommend that you talk together about how you can build prayer into your daily pattern of living.

In our own marriage, we have noticed how this pattern has changed as our circumstances have altered. Early in our marriage we used to enjoy a leisurely evening meal, during which we would talk about things that had happened at work that day. At the end of the meal we would spend a few minutes following a daily reading in the Bible and then praying together, usually covering the everyday things that were in our hearts. When our children were born and the demands of ministry increased, we found the pattern had to change. Now, for instance, the evening meal is *not* the most tranquil moment in a busy day. Trying to get a bit of holy stillness there is a miracle we have yet to achieve! We have developed a pattern where we meet once a week around a meal to read and pray together, and this has become a special time in our home. This means that our praying as a couple is usually done late at night. We confess it is not the best time to pray as our minds are tired, but it is often the quietest period of our day. We have tried not to get locked into a slavish system. Regularly, we will break off to pray together in the middle of the day, over the telephone or driving the car (with our eyes open, of course!). Some of our special times are when Ian is at home in his study and a mid-morning coffee break suddenly is turned into a prayer time.

Now we don't want you to feel defeated, nor do we wish to give the impression that we are a super-spiritual couple who have made it. We freely admit we often pray too little and talk too much. God has much to teach us in both departments. The point we wish to make is the more you make prayer part of life, the more your life will become one of prayer.

Reading the Bible together has been a source of blessing to many couples. Having tried all sorts of ideas, schemes and reading plans we have only one piece of advice: find what suits you and work at it. We have found that reading God's Word together has often helped us through hard times. It has been amazing to see how a particular Bible reading has exactly fitted circumstances we were facing. The Bible says of itself, 'The unfolding of your words gives light' (Ps. 119:130). There have been many occasions when we felt we were stumbling around in the dark and the Word of God has brought us direction.

As human beings we tend to function best within the patterns of routine. That is why we suggest that you aim at a regular time to pray and read the Bible together. If you fail to achieve it every day that does not mean God loves you any less. But if you have a goal that you are both aiming at, it will help you in your early years of marriage to build a strong spiritual relationship together.

## Belonging to a local church

Getting married can be a make-or-break time for many young Christian couples. The demands of marriage have turned some couples so inward on themselves that they have quickly drifted away from their commitment to the Lord Jesus. On the other hand, marriage has been a means of helping many young Christians towards a more clearly defined life of discipleship. There are various factors that account for this phenomenon, one of them being the issue of commitment to a local church.

We are increasingly finding that, due to economic pressure, young couples are having to move away from their home area simply because it is too expensive for them to live there. For a Christian couple this puts them in a dilemma. Do they try to find a church in their new area or face the complicated business of commuting several miles each Sunday back to their home church? If that is a question you are facing we suggest you talk it over carefully with your church leaders. They are responsible for your pastoral care and should be able to give you wise advice.

What if you are certain that you need to change churches? How do you set about finding the right one? How do you know when you have found it?

As with every major decision that you face as a couple, God invites you to seek his help. But he has given you brains to think with as well. In our own marriage we have twice been in the position of moving to a new area. We have asked the following questions as we have looked for a new spiritual home.

## Is this a church with spiritual life?

That may sound a terribly arrogant question but we believe it to be a valid one. As long as you are aware of the difference between spiritual *hype* and spiritual *life* you won't go far wrong. It takes time to penetrate the trappings of a church to get to its heart. Anyone can make a service look reasonably lively, but you will soon discover if that is a mere show. Beware of having a narrow view of spirituality. For example, we came from very conservative evangelical free churches, Ruth from a Brethren assembly and Ian from a Baptist church. Although we saw the shortcomings of both our traditions (as well as the strengths), God had to teach us much about the majesty of Anglican liturgy, the spontaneity of Pentecostalism, the glories of the Methodist hymnbook and the refreshing streams of charismatic renewal. Spiritual life is not the exclusive property of any one branch of the church. When you find it you will know it.

## Is this a church where
## the Word of God is taught?

One of the primary functions of any local church is to teach Christians to be effective disciples of Jesus in today's world. Sadly, some local churches relegate preaching and teaching to the bottom of their agendas. This is not the place to comment on this tragic failure other than to say that as a couple you need to find a church where you can be taught. A church with a high regard for preaching and teaching is usually a church with a high regard for Scripture as the Word of God. By attending services for a few weeks you will soon discover if this is a church where you will be spiritually fed.

You may have come from a church with a high standard of teaching and you feel disappointed that you are unable to find anywhere else to match this. We would encourage you not to be put off. The church you are joining may be at a different level of growth from your home church and because of this the level of teaching may have to be different. Also, not all ministers or leaders are gifted teachers. But if the Word of God is taught with faithfulness and prayer then God will honour it.

We are not to sit in church as sermon-samplers, giving marks out of ten for performance, star quality, content and the like. But if you are going to commit yourselves to be part of a local church it is essential that you find a place where you will grow.

## Is this a church with
## leaders of spiritual authority?

It is important to find a church which is led by godly leadership. Perhaps the church you are thinking of joining is of a different denomination or style from the one you are used to. That should not be a barrier because, as we have already suggested, God is not confined to one branch of the church, thankfully. This may mean that the leadership pattern is different in some ways. The question centres not so much on the style of running the church as on the Christian character and call of its leader or leaders.

There will come times in your married life when you will want to seek advice. Is this a church that can provide it? Do you believe that these leaders can take you forward in your discipleship? Is this local church being led with faith and vision? The answers to these questions will help you to determine the spiritual authority of the minister and other leaders.

## Is this a church where
### we can give as well as receive?

We do not believe that we should look at a local church solely on the basis of what we can get out of it. Rather, we should be asking what can we contribute to the life of this fellowship.

Large churches with successful reputations can be a drawback to spiritual growth if there is no outlet for service. Look carefully at the church you are considering joining and discover if there are areas of service that you would feel able to tackle as a couple. Serving together is one of God's ways to help us grow together.

Jim and Alison, for example, moved to a new town after their wedding. Their search for a new church led them to two very different alternatives. There was a large Anglican church in the town centre with a congregation of over 400, a good teaching ministry and a crowd of students and young marrieds. The second church was a small group of Christians meeting in a school on a council estate at the edge of town. This pioneer project had been started by the large Anglican church and they had sent twenty of their members across with a young curate. There were plans for a small church building to be erected eventually, but that was still a long way off.

Jim and Alison faced a tough choice. A large part of them wanted to join the lively and enthusiastic congregation in the town centre. They prayed and talked their decision through with great care. The thing that decided the matter for them was a verse they came across in their Bible reading. Jesus said, 'The Son of Man did not come to be served, but to serve, and to give his life as a ransom for many' (Mt. 20:28). They both recognized that they could easily become passengers in the larger church, but if they wanted to be servants, then the pioneer fellowship was the place to be.

Alison could see that her musical gifts could easily be used in the small church and Jim had spotted that the youth club badly needed a masculine presence to quell the weekly riots. A few years on, Alison has developed a small worship group and some of Jim's youth club have formed a weekly Bible study which the two of them lead. The church has moved a long way in a short time and, interestingly enough, so have Jim and Alison.

One final thing before we leave the subject of choosing a local church. If you are buying a house in a new area we advise you to look first for a local church. When most couples look for a new home they consider important factors such as the proximity of the schools and shopping centre. It seems to us to be a sensible thing first to find the church you intend joining, and then to start looking for a house within easy reach. This may sound impractical, but when you decide to start a family you will realize the benefits of living within the locality of your church, particularly if you do not have your own transport. We believe it is better to opt for a more modest choice of home and to be within the community where the church is based than to live in more luxurious but isolated surroundings.

## Giving

We express our love for God as much by our actions as by our words. That is why it is important, from the outset of your marriage, to get the discipline of regular financial giving straight. Even though you may find yourselves on a tight budget at first, giving to God must take a priority in your financial planning if you intend to honour him in your marriage. Here are some of the basic questions we are asked by couples who want to honour God in their financial affairs.

## How much?

For many Christians the principle of tithing (that is, giving a tenth of) their income has become a sacred duty. Personally, our own reading of the Old Testament showed us that tithing was the *minimum* laid upon the Israelite community; in reality their giving to God exceeded one tenth of their income. We believe the tithe principle is a helpful guideline, but it should not prevent us from more generous giving as God directs us. The issue of how much we should give needs to be decided, after prayer, together.

## How often?

This depends on your salary arrangements, whether you are paid weekly or monthly. Giving needs to be regular, systematic and planned, we believe. From our own experience, when we have relied on spontaneity rather than planned giving, the system has broken down. We have discovered the hard way that we function best within the discipline of a system.

## To whom?

Primarily our giving needs to be directed to the local church of which we are a part. Our commitment to a body of local Christians is expressed by our willingness to be involved financially in supporting the needs of that church. At the same time, through our giving we can be involved in God's wider church. Overseas mission, agencies involved in relief work and those engaged in specialized ministries in Britain among the young or within the inner cities all deserve financial support. Giving financially is a wonderful means of stimulating your prayer life as well. For several years we belonged to a British-based missionary organization and we discovered that our work simply could not have continued without the faithful prayers and financial support of Christians across Britain who were committed to stand with us in the work God called us to do. It is a thrilling experience to be a vital part of some larger work that God is doing, and you will discover that committed giving will allow you to become involved in his work.

We have discovered that giving is often a thermometer that indicates the state of our hearts. That is why we make no apology for including it in this chapter on spiritual growth. We are still learning the truth of the statement that 'growing Christians give and giving Christians grow'.

## Serving

Most visitors to the Holy Land visit the Dead Sea. Set in the desert wastes, its name seems most appropriate. The deadness of the sea is renowned because of its fatal effect upon fish. This is attributed to the concentration of chemical deposits which make the waters both extremely salty and buoyant. The sea is fed by the great River Jordan and four other fresh streams, but it has no outlet. Waters flow in, but nothing flows out. The water level is maintained through evaporation caused by the soaring temperatures.

The Dead Sea provides a powerful illustration for Christians who are always taking in and never giving out. It is a sure recipe for spiritual deadness. Serving God and serving others is the way to create a healthy outflow for your faith.

Marriage can become a terribly selfish trap if we are not careful. Becoming preoccupied with our home and with ourselves can rob us of leading balanced lives. Spiritual muscles are developed through exercise. Service for God can take many forms. It may well involve committing ourselves to a particular job within our local church, opening our home regularly for hospitality, getting involved within the community in a special project or giving time to an inter-church organization in our town. Make sure that you are learning to serve and ask God for specific ways to practise that.

## God is the gardener

On the night before the crucifixion Jesus shared a meal with his closest followers. Years later, as the men who attended that final meal looked back, they recalled the words and actions of that memorable night. John devotes several chapters of his gospel to an account of the evening.

Among other things that evening, Jesus spoke to his disciples about growth, and as he did so he used an example from the natural world to explain a truth about the spiritual world. Spiritual fruitfulness, according to Jesus, results from two distinct actions.

### God's part

The Father is the master gardener who knows that the way to ensure a fruitful vine is skilful yet radical pruning. The dead parts must be cut off and the fruitful ones cut back. This is the way to produce a bumper crop (see Jn. 15:1–8).

### Our part

Our part is to remain in him. This means staying in close fellowship with Jesus, who is the source of our strength. As the branch bears fruit because it is part of the vine, so we must remain rooted in Christ, allowing his life to flow through us. It is the fruit of his Spirit that we need to see produced in our lives (see Gal. 5:22ff.).

This represents two elements of a single truth rather like the two sides of a coin. Spiritual growth in your marriage depends, first, on the fact that God has committed himself to help you to become fruit-bearing followers of Jesus. His pruning action can take many forms. The discipline of disappointment, facing tough issues, the experience of failure or suffering can be things which, in the loving hands of God, can be used to increase our fruitfulness. Bishop J. C. Ryle once wrote: 'There is no gain without pain.' For the child of God, pain is never pointless but ultimately productive.

Second, you need dogged determination to remain close to the Lord Jesus Christ and obey him in every area of your life. He has promised that if we remain in him, his life-giving power will flow through our lives.

You may well experience difficult times in your married life when it would be easy to suppose that God has abandoned you. We share these twin principles of growth on the solid foundation of the truth of the Word of God. Often the hard times we encounter are a direct response to our prayer, 'Lord, make us better Christians.' In his loving wisdom God knows that pruning is the way to a greater harvest.

Most couples have a tape recording or video recording of their wedding service. If you have one, can we suggest that, from time to time, you play it back together? Listen carefully to the words of the hymns that you chose on that special day. Listen to the promises that you made before God to each other and hear again the prayers offered on your behalf. We are not suggesting that you do this merely as an exercise in nostalgia (although that's not a bad thing), but to help you recall the way in which you started out on married life in the presence of God. Those aspirations were not just for a one-hour service, but set out your intentions as you embarked upon marriage. Keep them before you and determine to live out your married life within his presence. There is no better way to find a fulfilled marriage than by staying close to the One who is its author.

# To those with
## non-Christian partners

We have written this chapter dealing with spiritual growth in marriage on the assumption that both husband and wife are committed Christians. We realize that some of our readers have a partner who is a non-Christian. A number of our friends have faced this situation, either now or at some stage in the past. By way of practical help we want to pass on some suggestions which our friends have shared with us from their experience.

## Pray

It may seem so obvious that it hardly has to be mentioned that you need to pray for your non-Christian partner. There may well be times when you feel frustrated at your partner's seemingly total lack of interest in Christian truth. At such times it is better to pray than argue. Read the parable Jesus told about the persistent widow (Lk. 18:1–8), and note carefully the introduction to the story: 'Then Jesus told his disciples a parable to show them that they should always pray and not give up.' Even when the going gets tough, God invites us to persist in prayer, because by our steadfastness we demonstrate our faith.

## Love your partner

You are more likely to make an impression on your partner by your actions than by your words. This is what Peter, one of the first Christian leaders, meant when he wrote about unbelieving husbands: 'They may be won over without words by the behaviour of their wives, when they see the purity and reverence of your lives' (1 Pet. 3:1–2).

We remember one Sunday night when Joy asked to see us after the evening service. After months of thinking things through, and due to the love and prayers of her close Christian friend, Joy wanted to give her life to the Lord Jesus Christ. It was quite obvious from what she said that her marriage to Terry was at breaking-point. She admitted to us that she was having an affair with a man at work, which she now realized must end if she was going to begin to follow Jesus. Within a few weeks Joy asked to be baptized and, having spent some time explaining to her what the New Testament has to say about this important step of discipleship, we advised her to go home and talk things over with Terry. She contacted us within a few days, very upset as Terry had made it quite clear he did not want her to get 'too religious' and was opposed to her being baptized. We advised her to let things ride and assured her that God would honour her willingness to respect her husband's views on this matter.

A few weeks later Joy arrived at church one Sunday flushed with excitement. Her words tumbled out: 'Terry says he is happy for me to be baptized and he has promised to come to the service as well!' We were curious to know what had made Terry change his mind. Joy explained that during a heart-to-heart conversation Terry had talked about the enormous change he had seen in her in just a few short weeks. Her attitude to him, to the children and even to the housework had drastically changed. 'I don't know what's happened to you,' he had told her, 'but I like it. You're a different person, and a nicer one at that!' Terry is much nearer the kingdom now than he was then because he has seen the lasting change in Joy's life.

We heard of a non-Christian husband whose enthusiastic wife kept leaving tracts around the house and used every spare moment to turn things into a 'spiritual conversation'. He wearily commented, 'It's like living with Billy Graham!' The wife (fortunately) had wise leaders in her local church who advised her to say less and do more. They even counselled her to attend fewer meetings at the church in order to spend more time with her husband. He came to faith in Jesus because the practice of Christianity in their home convinced him of the reality of his wife's faith.

Or take as another example Brian and Jo's story. Brian became a committed Christian through the influence of a friend at work. He and Jo have been happily married for a long time, and their children have all grown up and left home.

Initially, Jo was pleased that Brian had 'found something he's been looking for' as she described his decision to become a committed Christian. His new-found faith made no real difference to their social lives, and, to Jo's mind, Brian going to church on a Sunday morning was only the equivalent of friends' husbands choosing to play golf once a week.

But, as the months passed, tensions appeared in their relationship, and both Brian and Jo admitted they were in choppier waters than they had previously known in thirty years of marriage. Jo felt excluded and in some senses neglected. Brian felt misunderstood, and, at times, very alone.

It took some honesty on both their parts to face up to some important adjustments. At the moment Jo has not yet arrived at a point of saying she is a committed Christian, and there are a list of questions she is still working through. But she attends church with Brian on a semi-regular basis and has a more sympathetic understanding of his faith. On Brian's part, he has realized that following Christ includes aiming to be a better husband to Jo. Constantly attending Christian meetings is not the way to express that commitment to her, and he has realized that his responsibilities and interests need to be balanced. He has found enormous support from several friends in the church who have gone out of their way to make Jo feel welcome. In fact, they are planning to share a holiday in France with two other couples from the church, which is a positive step all round.

In each of these relationships, it is interesting to note that the Christian partners needed to realize that actions speak louder than words.

## Aim to grow

You need to aim to achieve a proper balance between your commitment to the Lord Jesus and your commitment to your partner. A number of our friends have commented that, at first, their non-Christian partners viewed their Christian commitment as a tremendous threat to the relationship. Wives have told us that husbands almost viewed Jesus as 'another man' who had intruded on the marriage. With love and reassurance this obstacle can be overcome. But you will need to work hard at maintaining the balance. For example, as a Christian you need fellowship and teaching to help you grow in your faith. The opposite danger to running too fast (and alienating your partner) is that of going too slow and becoming stunted in your own spiritual growth.

### Enlist others to pray

Our friends have told us about the encouragement they have received through the regular prayer support of other Christians. They have also admitted that, at times, they felt they were being disloyal to their partner in talking about their reactions behind their back. That is why it is good to have a small group of friends you can trust and ask them to stand with you in praying for your partner, without betraying your partner's trust or running him or her down.

If you belong to a house group or Bible study group then share your prayer needs with the others in the group and ask them to support you in regular prayer.

### Let God do it his way

We wish we had sufficient space to tell you a few of the remarkable testimonies of some of our friends who have now become complete as Christian couples. In some cases it has taken years of faithful prayer and witness before that breakthrough has been achieved. One of the things that fascinates us as we have been recalling some of these stories is that God has brought those non-Christian partners to a living faith in Jesus in his own way and in his own time. For instance, we can think of those who, despite having attended special evangelistic events and the like, have committed their lives to Christ quite independently. God can speak to your partner outside of a Christian meeting, so don't limit his ability to work.

A common trap that Christians in this situation fall into is trying to engineer events to bring your partner into a situation where he or she will be converted. Non-Christians may be Christless but they are not brainless. Sometimes the very manipulating of circumstances can produce a heart resistant to the message. Prayer, faith and a lot of love will work more wonders than any amount of plotting.

## Have faith

The Bible says of Abraham, 'Against all hope, Abraham in hope believed' (Rom. 4:18). His life is an example of how to battle on in faith even when the circumstances are stacked against you. Humanly speaking, the odds against Abraham ever having a son by his wife Sarah were overwhelming. But against all hope, Abraham believed. We sincerely trust that you do not feel as despondent as Abraham must have done at times. But having prayed, supported and encouraged many friends who have stood where you are standing now, we pass on what we have said to them many times: 'Trust God; he's big enough.'

You have a natural concern for your partner to come to know Jesus. How much greater God's love is for him or her as an individual and for you both as a couple. We pray that God will give you the grace to keep on keeping on, and that he will give you strong Christian friends who will stand with you as you trust God.

## Notes

[1] Mike and Katey Morris, *Praying Together* (Kingsway, 1987).
[2] *Ibid*, p. 17.

# CHAPTER SIX

# LOVING
## AND LEARNING

We remember reading a cartoon in a newspaper. A young couple were sitting up in bed, their suitcase with a 'Just Married' sticker clearly visible and clothes strewn across the floor. There was a mystified look on their faces and the caption simply read: 'Well . . . was that it?'

We found it struck a chord because, as children of the 'swinging sixties', we found ourselves feeling a little let down when we first made love. The earth didn't move and there were no violins or crashing breakers of surf to enrich the occasion.

Within western society, human sexuality has been used, abused, glamorized and distorted beyond measure. When sex is used to sell double glazing it merely demonstrates that, as a society, we have lost our sense of what is truly valuable.

But just as the world (or at least part of it) has overrated sex, we must quickly admit that at times through the centuries the Christian church has been guilty of undervaluing it. A woman can be debased as much by a cynical attitude as by a pornographic photograph. The Christian church seems quick to oppose pin-up pictures but woefully slow to challenge insidious chauvinism within its ranks.

Living in a world where, sex is the subject of overkill, Christians sometimes find themselves swinging to the opposite extreme of devaluing one of God's choicest gifts to humanity. Sexuality is good. God created men and women with sexual bodies and sexual appetites. But as with all of his gifts, it comes complete with a set of instructions. Within God's guidelines it is a gift which brings deep and lasting fulfilment. Flout the rules and you spoil the gift.

God's guidelines set out that sexual intercourse is a gift to be used within the commitment of a marriage relationship, between a man and a woman, and that faithfulness within that sexual relationship is to be maintained (see Heb. 13:4; 1 Cor. 6:18–20; Gn. 2:24–25). More than anyone else, Christian couples should be able to enjoy sexual fulfilment within marriage as a part of God's design for living. There is no reason to feel guilty or ashamed about your sex life as a couple; it is God's loving intention that you should both enjoy his gift to the full.

A piece of research in the USA some years ago revealed that a couple committed to faithfulness in marriage and firm religious convictions are the highest percentage group reporting a fulfilling sex life – which seems to fly in the face of the distorted image of Christians being freaky fundamentalists who find sex distasteful.

In this chapter we want to examine how we can build a satisfying physical relationship. One thing our cartoon characters had obviously not been told is that sex is a growing process. As you learn to love so your understanding of one another develops. If the honeymoon proves to be a sexual let-down, don't despair; practice makes perfect!

## A fresh start

We want to begin by tackling a subject that is often brought up by couples contemplating marriage. Statistics vary greatly, but it is estimated that the majority of newly-weds are not virgins on their wedding night. We have come across a significant number of people who, in their pre-Christian days, have had various sexual partners. The question is often asked, 'How much do I tell my partner about my previous sexual experience?'

Assuming that you have understood that the basis of God's forgiveness is repentance (breaking with sin) and faith in Jesus Christ, you need to consider your partner's personality very carefully. As a general rule, we believe it is right for a couple to talk about past sexual encounters simply because a strong relationship needs to be based on honesty and frankness. The advent of Aids has resulted in people needing to be far more up front with their partner about previous sexual activity, in order that health risks can be minimized. For this and several other reasons, we think it is good for a couple to be open with each other, although it is not particularly help-full to go into details. If we are not careful we can end up feeding our partner's insecurities, so the advice we give is to share about the past with openness but also with sensitivity. If you are unsure about what to do, ask someone who is a trusted friend, or a leader in your local church. We recognize that not all relationships can cope with the shock of revelation from the past, and that is why calling someone alongside to advise is the best course of action.

Sin is a terrible thing. Once its tentacles have wrapped themselves around someone, it is only the power of the Lord Jesus Christ that can set them free. Even when we think the past has been covered and dealt with, guilt can invade our quiet consciences. If you are battling with the problem of guilt, we would encourage you to seek help. It is God's intention that you should live as a free person, not bound by the past.

We recall a friend called Penny telephoning us one day, obviously distraught. She and her husband, Robin, were a happily married couple in their forties with three teenage children. They were both active members of their local church and appeared to be a couple whose love was growing deeper all the time. Penny came round to see us and she was very upset. She told us that in her time at university she had mixed with a fairly lively set. She did the minimum of work and spent most of her time drinking, partying and generally sleeping around. Her promiscuous lifestyle had left her empty and unfulfilled. Penny's search for meaning eventually led her to open her life to Christ and, for the first time, she discovered the release of forgiveness. A few years later she met Robin and they soon knew they were made for each other. They could now look back on almost twenty years of happy married life together. Penny told us that before they were married she had talked to Robin about her promiscuous lifestyle at university. He was understanding and had hardly ever referred to those far-off days throughout their marriage.

Penny's dilemma had been caused because of an abortion she had undergone in the middle of her time at university. Having discovered she was pregnant, and not knowing who the father could be, she had confided in a friend who helped her to make the necessary arrangements with a private clinic. When Penny became a Christian she knew that this abortion was one of the areas of her life she needed to confess and put right with God. Apart from occasional twinges of guilt when her own children were conceived, she had never really been troubled by this episode from the past. Then suddenly the abortion debate filled the newspapers. A new Bill was before parliament, the papers took up the debate in columns of newsprint and Christians began to voice concerns about the moral issues involved. The pro-life argument had become a major concern in their local church, and Penny found herself becoming deeply disturbed. She had joined a counselling team within her church, and it seemed almost every week she was being faced by women racked with guilt because of having undergone abortions.

Penny suddenly lost her sense of direction. Although she had been frank with Robin about the past, she had never told him about her abortion. Her feelings of guilt were such that she began to withdraw from the physical side of their relationship. She became impatient with the children and her Christian life seemed to be in ruins. In desperation she telephoned us that day, realizing she could not go another hour without bringing this secret from the past out into the open.

As soon as Penny told us her story the weight began to lift from her shoulders. Her frank confession actually removed the power of the accusation from her conscience. We counselled and prayed with her over specific things, but, in one sense, most of the work was done by Penny herself. Instead of living with a guilty secret she chose to take God's way out (see Jas. 5:16).

None of us needs to live as prisoners of the past. By repressing guilt and trying to shut off the memories of yesterday, we can actually create pressures in the present. The promise of Jesus still stands: 'If the Son sets you free, you will be free indeed' (Jn. 8:36).

## Learning to love

Sexual intercourse is the most intimate expression of a human relationship. Unfortunately, for some, it is regarded as nothing more than a physical activity, as can be seen by glancing at some of the books available on the subject. God designed the act of sexual intercourse as a unique act of loving, involving our whole being, mental, emotional and spiritual, as well as the physical dimension. He intends it to be something which draws a husband and wife close together and, because of this, it is an act of love to be enjoyed by a couple within the commitment of a marriage relationship.

We like the expression 'making love' not only because it sounds less clinical than 'sexual intercourse' but also because it describes what a satisfying physical relationship can achieve, making the bond of marriage stronger and deeper. Human beings are complex creations and human sexuality powerfully illustrates that. Building your physical relationship together is enriching and a wonderful means of bringing you closer to one another. Learning to love can be an exciting dimension of marriage. As with any learning process it is helpful to get the facts straight, and that is why we recommend to every couple the purchase of a good book which deals in detail with the sexual side of marriage. In recent years a number of well-written books have been produced by Christian publishers. Three we particularly recommend are Tim and Beverley La Haye, *The Act of Marriage*, Ed and Gaye Wheat, *Intended for Pleasure*, and John and Janet Houghton, *A Touch of Love*. (See p. 192 for details.)

When we were first married there were no such books on the Christian scene. After a furtive look around the shelves of our local bookshop we managed to find one written by an eminent doctor, but it dealt with sexuality from a purely humanistic viewpoint, which meant we needed to filter its advice very carefully. We are glad that over recent years several books have appeared which set the enjoyment of sex within marriage in a Christian framework.

A couple who have been married for some years could also find such books helpful in developing the sexual side of marriage. Thankfully, the learning process is not confined to the honeymoon; it goes on throughout marriage. To read through such a book together can be a starting-point to discuss your different needs and responses. As we will mention later, being willing to talk together freely about such things is a great way to overcome problems and learn to understand each other better.

We realize that some people reading this book will find the thought of consulting an explicit sex manual unnecessary or even embarrassing. Perhaps they take the view that sex is simply a case of 'doing what comes naturally'. It is worth pointing out that in our own experience, and in the experience of others engaged in counselling married couples, many of us need help in discovering the joys of sex. After all, most of us need lessons to drive a car or install a central heating system, and we think you will agree that a fulfilling sexual relationship is more important than either of these!

## Family planning

We want to look in this section at the question of contraception. This is a subject on which Christians have taken differing views over the years. For example, the Roman Catholic Church takes a very strong line against any form of 'artificial contraception', as it is known. Other Christian groups within the Protestant church hold a similar view, teaching that a couple should trust God with regard to the conception of children. It is our personal belief that contraception, as with many other discoveries of medical science, is a gift of God and, as such, can be used as an enrichment of life.

One of the primary purposes of marriage is to procreate – that is, to bear children. The Bible gives a number of reasons for raising children.

*Fulfilling God's command.* God's first command to humanity is the command to be fruitful and multiply (Gn. 1:28). Raising children within the framework of a family is not to be seen as an act to please ourselves but as a fulfilment of God's direct instructions.

*Children are a blessing.* There are references throughout the Old Testament that equate the birth of children (especially sons) as a direct blessing from God (Ps. 127:4–5). The birth of a child was a time of special thanksgiving to God.

*Children are an expression of becoming 'one flesh'.* A child is a unique combination of the parents who produced it. To be conceived is something in which none of us had a choice, but it was the act of a man and a woman expressing the ultimate truth of the biblical statement, 'they will become one flesh' (Gn. 2:24).

What does all this mean to a childless couple? Should we consider them disobedient to God's commands, or regard them as being punished by him for something one (or both) of them has done or failed to do? We do not think so. There are usually medical or practical reasons why a couple remain childless. We can think of some of our friends who, for a variety of reasons, are childless yet enjoy a happy marriage. But it must be said that raising children is seen in the Bible as the norm for a married couple. This does not make a childless couple in any way abnormal, but rather they are a special case in God's eyes. We believe they become candidates for God's special blessings, as does a single person who remains unmarried throughout his or her life either by choice or circumstances. It is important to stress this, as there are instances when a married couple with a family fail to appreciate the unkind attitudes we sometimes hold towards those who have been led by God along a pathway different from our own.

We believe it is important that a couple should openly discuss their attitudes about having children, ideally before they are married. Rather than just 'letting things happen naturally' it is better to plan a family. The Bible does not stipulate how many children a couple should expect to produce. According to medical science, a healthy woman *could* produce as many as twenty children. The *Guinness Book of Records* tells us of the amazing Mr and Mrs Vassilet, from the Soviet Union, who produced sixty-nine children, including sixteen pairs of twins, seven sets of triplets and four sets of quadruplets. We are not told what this energetic couple did in their spare time!

Most couples we have talked with have a set idea of the number of children they would like. Modern family planning methods help us to realize those plans and determine the best time for a child to be born.

Contraception is a means to planning a family effectively and needs to be carefully considered by both partners. There are a number of ways in which you can find some advice on this matter:

- Read some of the books and literature available on the subject of family planning. (See the useful addresses at the end of the book.)
- Make an appointment to see your doctor or go direct to your local Family Planning Clinic. (Your local telephone directory will give you the address and telephone number.)
- Talk to your minister or local church leaders if you need more specific Christian teaching on the subject. Often they will know of a Christian doctor who may be better able to answer your questions.

It is important that you consider the various options together. For a husband simply to leave it to his wife to sort out the question of contraception is an abandonment of his responsibilities.

## Methods of birth control

### Which to choose?

In recent years trends have changed in contraception with a move to safer, more reliable methods. Advances m medical science have alerted the public to the long-term side-effects of certain drugs, and growing understanding of HIV has encouraged the increased use of the condom. This acts as a barrier which reduces the risk of infection during intercourse, as well as avoiding pregnancy.

A visit to your local Family Planning Clinic will provide you with various booklets and pamphlets which describe in helpful detail the methods of contraception available. Having read through their material in writing this book, we were impressed by the quality and scope of the service they offer.

What we have attempted to do is to set out some of the questions you might want to ask as you assess the wealth of information that groups like the Family Planning Association provide.

*Effectiveness.* Some methods have a greater failure rate than others. How important is it that you avoid getting pregnant now? Check the success rate of the method that you prefer.

*Suitability.* How convenient is a particular method? Does it suit your lifestyle? Is it practical?

*Risks and benefits.* If you are opting to use a method for several years, does this raise any health problems? Are there known long-term side effects?

*How is it used?* Some methods require a visit to the doctor, others involve devices that need to be fitted as you are about to make love. Does this affect your rating of a particular contraceptive's suitability?

*How does it work?* This is a critical question as it raises a number of important moral questions. Does this particular method square with my principles and beliefs?

## Contraceptive methods

There are five main categories of contraceptive methods. Here is a summary of each of them.

*Mechanical methods.* These prevent the man's sperm being introduced into the woman's uterus and Fallopian tubes. They include the condom (male and female versions) and the intra-uterine device (IUD).

*Chemical methods.* These prevent a woman's ovaries producing eggs each month. They also thicken the cervical mucus, making it difficult for the male sperm to enter, and make the lining of the woman's womb less likely to accept a fertilized egg. Included in this group are the pill (in a variety of forms and brand names) and the Depo-Provera injection.

*Permanent methods.* These prevent either sperm being produced in a man or eggs in a woman. This would involve a vasectomy for a man or sterilization for a woman.

*Natural methods.* These involve planning to have

intercourse during the so-called 'safe' periods in a woman's monthly cycle, or a man withdrawing himself from the woman's vagina just before his orgasm. Either way, the method is down to human planning and self-control.

*Post-coital methods.* This relatively new area of development in the field of contraception is one that poses a moral dilemma for many people. 'Post-coital' means 'after intercourse'. The method deals with any fertilized eggs and includes things such as the 'morning-after pill' and abortion. The main area of concern centres on the fact that it is, potentially at least, destroying rather than preventing life.

## What is on offer?

Within these five categories there is an increasing range of brand products. If you feel confused by the choices on offer, you will realize why we suggest that a visit to a Family Planning Clinic will help. Here is a summary of the main options in each category, with an indication as to their effectiveness.

### Mechanical methods

*Intra-uterine device (IUD):* 96–99% effective
>   Doctor must insert and remove it
>   Can be left in place for up to 5 years
>   Very small risk of pregnancy
>   Some risk of discomfort and bleeding
>   Some risk of infection
>   Does not minimize HIV risk

*Diaphragm and caps:* 85–97% effective
>   Can be fitted by the woman herself, after instruction
>   Has some risk, which can be minimized by using spermicide cream
>   Can be inserted well in advance of love-making
>   Does not minimize HIV risk

*Condoms:* 85–98% effective

If used properly, can be very effective

Principle objection is that it prevents spontaneity and naturalness

Minimizes risk of HIV

## Chemical methods

*Oral contraceptive pill:* 98–99% effective

Comes in two main varieties and various brand names

Convenient and easy to use

Despite various health scares, 'the pill' is used by nearly half of all women in the UK under 30 years of age

Very effective

(There are a list of things that your doctor will want to check before prescribing the pill. These relate to your current health, family medical history and previous health record.)

*Depo-Provera injection:* 99% effective

Given every 12 weeks by a doctor

Removes fear of forgetting to take the pill

Risk of pregnancy is extremely low

Normally used only as a short-term method

After-effects take up to a year to reduce after last injection

*Hormone implants:* 99.8% effective

An under-the-skin implant inserted by a doctor

Effective for 5 years, sometimes longer

A good long-term contraceptive which can easily be removed, whereupon fertility quickly returns

Very low failure rate

Some people have side effects (sickness, headaches, *etc.*)

No protection against HIV

## Permanent methods

*Female sterilization:* 1:300 failure rate

Can now be performed in day surgery

Must be performed under general anaesthetic by a surgeon

*Male sterilization:* 1:1,000 failure rate

Vasectomy can be performed under local or general anaesthetic, by a doctor

Quick and efficient with a high success rate

The fact that both of these options are described as permanent shows that they are usually employed when a couple decide they do not wish to have any more children. Although neither operation is always irreversible, careful thought must be given before proceeding, to make sure there are no regrets later.

## Natural methods

*Rhythm method:* high risk of pregnancy

The woman determines the fertile and infertile times in her cycle

Intercourse is limited to the 'safe' (infertile) time of the month

Needs a fair degree of skill and patience

Can be very frustrating when you want to make love and can't

Can create unnecessary anxiety for both partners

Natural, involving no drugs or devices

*Withdrawal method:* high risk of pregnancy

The man withdraws his penis before orgasm

Can be less than satisfying for both partners

Not a 'safe' method

Involves a great deal of determination

## Post-coital methods

*'Morning-after' contraception*

This is sometimes described as emergency contraception, because it is taken after the event of sexual intercourse.

There are two main methods:

> Insertion of IUD by a doctor
>
> A combination '2-dose' pill

The latter carries a higher health risk as it contains a hormone dose much higher than that contained in the contraceptive pill.

*Abortion, or termination of pregnancy*

> A surgical procedure to terminate a pregnancy

(From our personal point of view, we do not believe that post-coital methods are an acceptable form of contraception. They are included here by way of explanation only.)

## Infertility

For some couples the issue is not how to prevent pregnancy, but how to become pregnant. We can think of several close friends who have struggled with that heartbreaking problem. It is worth saying something on the subject at this point. Even if it does not apply to you as a couple, there may be someone in your circle of contacts who is living with the pain of infertility.

People who long for children, yet for one reason or another cannot have them, carry extra pressures. These include the pressure of other people's expectations, the pressure of friends who are able to enjoy having babies with seeming ease, the pressure of ongoing medical tests, the pressure of thinking everyone is talking about you, the pressure of disappointment and the pressure of feeling that God has let you down.

More than anything else, couples faced with these pressures need friends who will love, pray and care for them.

As we sit and write, we can think of several couples once declared infertile who are now living with the joy of miracle children. We can also think of others who have recognized that God has another plan for their lives. They have gone for this not as a second best, but with faith and joy.

But with both groups, we can see how real love and friendship has carried them through a difficult time in their married lives.

## First attempts at making love

According to Woody Allen, 'There are only two things in life that are important. One is sex ... and the other is not all that important.' That probably sums up the attitude of many of us as engaged couples eagerly looking forward to marriage.

First attempts at making love can be great fun, provided that your expectations are such that you don't plan to become experts in a fortnight. Remember the advice we were given: one thing for newly-weds to pack for their honeymoon is a sense of humour. If you can learn to develop a relaxed and open attitude towards sex you will discover years of uninhibited enjoyment within your relationship together.

Inside a woman's vaginal passage is a membrane (or skin) which needs to be broken before full intercourse can take place. This is called the hymen, and when it is intact it confirms virginity. For some women, the normal activities of life have caused this membrane to be broken, but for others sexual intercourse will make this happen. As the man's erect penis is introduced to the woman's vagina the act of penetration will cause the hymen to break. The membrane barrier usually breaks quite easily although it causes a small amount of bleeding and will be slightly painful for the woman. That is why the man needs to be careful and gentle in his initial penetration and will need the help of his partner's hands to guide his penis into position.

In a few cases, a woman may need an internal examination by a doctor to break her hymen. If you are concerned about this, especially if you have never used tampons, consult your doctor or the Family Planning Clinic.

Some couples experience difficulty in breaking the hymen initially and, if that is the case, it is best to be patient and try to complete full intercourse the next day saving embarrassment and discomfort. There is no law that says you should achieve full intercourse on your wedding night and, after all the excitement of the big day, you may just as well prefer to cuddle and kiss before getting a good night's sleep. If problems about penetration continue, you need to consult a doctor. Although you may feel embarrassed about this, remember that a professional doctor will have dealt with all sorts of similar situations during his or her career and, in the right sense of the phrase, you are 'just another patient'.

It is not always easy for a man either. He may experience some discomfort if the foreskin of his penis is too tight when he has an erection or if the foreskin becomes pulled back during intercourse. This can be painful as the foreskin protects the very sensitive area at the tip of his penis. For men who have been circumcised (that means that their foreskins have been removed by minor surgery) this is not a problem. If any difficulties persist, seek medical advice.

The use of a good lubricant (there are several non-greasy brands available from chemists' shops) will ease penetration. The man can apply this to his penis and the woman to the lips of her vagina. It may sound terribly messy and unromantic, but in the context of pleasing and loving each other it can be applied without destroying a romantic atmosphere.

We have already discussed the differences between men and women and these are even more apparent in the area of sexual response. Much has been written on the subject and the Christian-based sex manuals we recommended earlier in this chapter have some very helpful things to say about the differing needs and responses of the sexes.

The old-fashioned notion that all men are interested in is sex and all a woman can do is grin and bear it has, thankfully, been put to rest. The truth is that God created men and women as sexual beings. Environment, education (or lack of it) and experiences mould our attitudes to sex for better or worse. We need to understand our partner and ourselves if we are going to explore the deepest joys of sexual love.

For a woman, the right atmosphere, tenderness, loving words and caresses mean a great deal. Although a man may find it difficult to understand fully, a woman can be just as sexually satisfied sometimes by a prolonged cuddling session as by intercourse itself.

Men, on the other hand, tend to be more sexually impulsive. Orgasm is the goal and a man finds his release in the act of ejaculation. Learning to understand each other's different needs at various times will take patience and understanding from both of you.

We once heard a brilliant description of the difference in sexual responses in men and women. A friend of ours described a woman as being like an electric oven; it takes a long time to warm up, but once it does, it stays hot for a long time. A man, by contrast, is like a gas cooker; it takes no time to heat up, and cools down almost immediately.

One last word of advice on the subject of first attempts at making love. Don't set standards too high for yourselves. You have a lifetime to share together, and although the films and glossy magazines may tell you that you are a failure if you are not an Olympic athlete in sex at the first go, life simply is not like that. A fulfilling sex life is like a long journey. In the first year you will only cover a few miles and some of the country you discover may seem flat and uninteresting. But as the journey continues and you develop a deeper joy in your companionship you will also discover a depth of intimacy you never dreamt was possible. The landscape gets more interesting the further you travel. We read in the book of Genesis: 'The man and his wife were both naked, and they felt no shame' (Gn. 2:25). That refers, we believe, not just to physical nakedness but also to complete openness emotionally, mentally and spiritually. They were able to reveal everything of themselves to each other without shame, because of the security of love. Carry that with you on your journey and you will discover joy.

## Some common problems

Every couple soon discovers that marriage means learning to give as well as take. In the sexual side of a relationship this is proved to be true. When the marriage service refers to taking each other 'for better or worse' it makes it plain that your marriage will face good times and, on occasions, bad times as well. In your sexual relationship you will encounter some not-so-easy times. Pressure at work, pregnancy or broken nights with a baby cutting its first set of teeth can make romance evaporate. At such times extra love is needed by both partners. There may be occasions when you don't feel like making love but you will do it because you want to please your partner. Similarly, there may come times when you want to make love, but you will read from your partner's signals that he or she is exhausted. So you put aside your own wants in the other's best interests. That is what it means to be a giver, and givers make the best lovers.

We thought it would be useful to note some of the problems that occur from time to time in the sexual lives of couples. None is without solution, and knowing about them will at least help you towards a clearer understanding of sexuality.

### Impotence

This is when a man is unable to achieve an erection or maintain it sufficiently to enable full sexual intercourse to take place. There are a number of possible causes, including tiredness, depression, anxiety or even guilt. Some men find at certain times in their lives they are victims of a temporary form of impotence and others suffer from it as a long-term problem. It can be tackled effectively in either case, provided the man is willing to seek help. This may mean a visit to the doctor or seeking expert counselling. Sex therapy is a perfectly respectable form of counselling and doesn't involve attending kinky parties! Your doctor, counsellor or minister will be able to advise you.

### Infection

Women are susceptible to vaginal infection which causes irritation and discharge. This can be easily treated with a cream or pessaries (or both) obtained from your GP. Such infections give an offensive smell and irritation and can also be passed on to your husband, so prompt action is needed.

### Premature ejaculation

This is when a man is unable to control the timing of his climax and ejaculates too soon. In the early stages of developing a sexual relationship some men find this a persistent problem, partly because they are just getting familiar with the feelings surrounding intercourse. Once a man can learn to read the signs, he can control his own actions to delay his climax until his wife is ready for the full act. There is a series of exercises that have been developed for couples to use to help a man to learn to control his timing. A few weeks of practice can not only help you overcome the problem but can be fun as well. Gaye and Ed Wheat's book, *Intended for Pleasure* (pp. 85–93), provides details of what is called the 'squeeze control technique' and is well worth careful reading.

### Failure to achieve orgasm

Some women find difficulty in achieving orgasm for a variety of reasons. Sometimes this is easily corrected with some practical information and muscle control. For others, there are perhaps more complex reasons that lie behind a woman's inability to find full sexual release. If as a wife you are experiencing difficulty in this area we would suggest you take the following steps:

- Read through a helpful book detailing a woman's sexual response. The books we have suggested deal thoroughly with the subject.
- Talk over with your husband how you find yourself turned on when making love. There will be certain things he can do to assist you towards a climax, and there may be certain things he is doing that are not helping you.
- Learn to relax and give yourself to your husband in your love-making. The less inhibited you are, the greater your own sexual feelings will become.
- Most women find being stimulated by their husband's hands or fingers in the clitoral area helps them considerably towards orgasm. This is not strange, but quite normal. You need to let your husband know you want this to happen.

If, after all this, you are still unable to achieve orgasm, then consult your doctor or Family Planning Clinic who will be able to put you in touch with someone who can provide more detailed help.

## Monthly periods

Every woman knows the hassle and monthly discomfort of her period. But for most men, marriage is the first head-on encounter with the complexities of the female menstrual cycle. The fact that as a woman you are off limits for a few days each month needs to be explained; don't assume he will simply understand. You need to talk about the way you feel at this time of the month. A mature man will cope with your need for a bit of special loving care at such times, but don't forget to reassure him that your love for him doesn't go round in a circle as well. At these times in the month you can still express your love for each other in different ways and, if you follow the principle of learning to serve your partner, you will both learn how to cope.

## Love-making during pregnancy

There is no medical reason why a couple should not continue to enjoy love-making throughout pregnancy. Obviously there are physical factors that make intercourse a little more difficult, but there is nothing that love and a sense of humour cannot overcome. Many of the books dealing with pregnancy tackle the question of sex and will allay any fears you might have about intercourse damaging the baby in any way.

We have discovered through four pregnancies that a woman's sexual drive is more closely linked with her general emotional state than a man's. During pregnancy a woman passes through a number of psychological barriers. At times she feels exceptionally tearful. One day she can be brimful of energy, the next she may want to sleep all day. She sometimes feels lumpy and a little like a misshapen bag of potatoes. She finds it hard to keep wearing the same old clothes each day, and at times feels like punching the next person who tells her she looks absolutely radiant and in the peak of health. She may, on occasions, feel panic-stricken at the thought of labour pains and the responsibility of becoming a mother. At other moments she will long with a physical ache to hold that bundle of new life she has nurtured within her for so many months. In short, your wife is being prepared for motherhood and there is more to it than incubating an egg for nine months.

A man does not need to be a professor in psychology to realize that, at this important stage in her life, his wife needs several basic things which he is best able to provide: love, security, reassurance and understanding. Telling her she looks beautiful when she is pregnant (and that she looks nothing like a sack of potatoes) will help her morale.

We have discovered that love-making during pregnancy can actually take on a special dimension. After all, can you think of a better way to provide love, security, reassurance and understanding?

## Developing sexual
## enjoyment in marriage

Not long ago we were sharing in a prayer time with a group of close friends. We went round the group detailing things that we wanted to thank God for in our lives in the recent past. The usual list of answers to prayer and the like were dutifully recited, then a close acquaintance brought a refreshing burst of honesty to the proceedings when he announced that he and his wife wanted to thank God that, after fourteen years of marriage, their physical relationship was getting better all the time. They were not showing off, but simply being honest about an area of their life that was a great joy to them both. That incident served to challenge us to thank God for all his good gifts and never to be ashamed of stating it (although we would advise you to pick your audience carefully).

Are there specific ways in which we can build a healthy and fulfilling sexual relationship? It seems to us that there are.

One question that frequently arises concerns how often a couple should make love. Our usual reply is: as often as you feel like it. Every couple has different responses, and within a marriage each partner has varying capacities for sex, depending on factors such as the time of the month, pressures of work, general health and tiredness. Some couples enjoy intercourse every day, whereas others find they manage quite satisfactorily on once or twice a week. There are no fixed rules on the subject that make you normal or abnormal. You need to decide together what suits you and your lifestyle best. As long as you realize that sex is not something you give or withhold as a reward or punishment, and provided you hold fast to the principle of giving yourself to your partner, you will find it easy to adjust to each other. Some people have a higher sex drive than their partners and both parties must take such things into account.

There is nothing sacred or spiritual about making love at bedtime. In fact, that can prove to be the worst time of the day if you are both exhausted. Nor does the Bible say that a bed is the only place for love-making, or that keeping the lights on or off is the best way to do it. Learning to be adventurous about the location, atmosphere and sexual positions helps to stimulate your love life. Clearly there are some areas of sexual experimentation that are morally wrong for Christians. But sexual enjoyment in marriage is a wonderful gift that God wants us to explore and enjoy to the full. Read through the Song of Solomon and you will realize that God, in placing this book within the Bible, does not have a narrow or puritanical view of human sexuality.

Atmosphere can do a great deal to boost your sex drive. A romantic evening for two at home or a special weekend away can help to fuel the fires of passion. Learn to be creative and adventurous together.

The New Testament teaches that a married couple should not withhold sex from each other 'except by mutual consent and for a time, so that you may devote yourselves to prayer. Then come together again so that Satan will not tempt you because of your lack of self-control' (I Cor. 7:5). Many couples have found it to be true that abstinence makes the heart grow fonder. Work commitments may enforce separation on you for a time and, provided that everything is kept in proper balance, this can actually serve to increase your enjoyment of each other rather than impairing it.

We have already emphasized that good communication is essential for building a strong marriage. This is particularly true in the area of sexual fulfilment. Take regular opportunities to talk over your sexual relationship with each other, explain to your partner what excites you most and ask them to be honest about their own needs. If you find it embarrassing to talk openly in this way at first, then try writing love notes to each other. Some of us find it easier to express our feelings on paper when we can think carefully about what we are writing. There is nothing dirty about this. On the contrary, it can prove to be a very intimate and special thing between the two of you. Keep the lines of communication open at all times and share your feelings. Choose your moments with care, as well as your words, because a bad sense of timing can create hurt. Half-way through making love is not the best time to tackle some matters.

Appearance is very important when it comes to making love. Take time over the way you look (and smell!), and that will communicate to your partner that you are doing more than performing a physical function.

We are continually learning that tender words and tender actions go together. Men, in particular, seem to have a problem in this area, possibly because it is not thought to be particularly macho to be a romantic. It is amazing how words can have a positive or negative effect on partners' responsiveness to each other. If you can learn to put the words of love and the actions of love together you will discover a deeper level of intimacy.

Yale psychologist Robert Sternberg undertook a study analysing the complex chemistry of what we call 'love'. He defined three key ingredients: intimacy, passion and commitment. He spelt out the meaning of all three. *Passion* is the quickest to develop and the quickest to fade. *Intimacy* develops more slowly and *commitment* more gradually still. All of this means that no relationship is stable because the basic components change at different rates. People don't know what they are in for when they fall in love. The divorce rate is so high, not because people make foolish choices, but because they are drawn together for reasons that matter less and less as time goes on. You may agree with us that this is a sad, pessimistic reflection of today's world. But Sternberg's analysis that the three components of love are *intimacy*, *passion* and *commitment* bears a close resemblance to what the Bible teaches as God's pattern for marriage. But in contrast the Bible indicates that these three things need not fade and die like autumn leaves.

With God's care we can nurture them and see love grow into the strong, vibrant force it was created to be: a mirror image of Christ's love for the church (see Eph. 5:25–30).

Sexual intimacy within marriage, far from being a sub-Christian, unspiritual activity, can actually draw us to the clearest human picture of the love of God that we can discover. Have fun practising!

# CHAPTER SEVEN

# BUILDING
## A HOME

When a young couple are struggling hard to put their home together they can easily fall into the trap of thinking, 'If only ...'. 'If only we had enough money for a new three-piece suite', or 'If only we could afford a proper holiday this year.' The truth is that even if all our 'if onlys' came true overnight they would not automatically bring us happiness.

It is worth remembering that some of the world's loneliest people live in the loveliest houses. You may have a living-room right out of the pages of a Sunday supplement, and still find it cold and empty. *People* make a home, not furniture. Russell Miller, in his book *The House of Getty*, details the life of Paul Getty, at one time the world's richest man. He makes the penetrating comment, 'All the sons of the richest man in the world could claim, with some justification, was that their father's fabulous wealth had brought them precious little joy.'

Jesus Christ uttered the warning: 'Watch out! Be on your guard against all kinds of greed; a man's life does not consist in the abundance of his possessions' (Lk. 12:15). In a society that lives by the motto 'you are what you have', it is good to know that, in God's economy, what you are is more important than what you own.

Thinking about some of the homes we have visited as a couple we have discovered that the places that are real homes have more than deep-pile carpets and stylish furniture. It is said that homes reflect the personalities of the people who live there. Where there are love, life and laughter it shows. And equally where there are tensions, tears and trauma, it is very obvious. In this chapter we are considering the ways in which you can, with God's help, build a home together. A home reflects your personalities but at the same time should convey something of his love for the world. You don't need pipe-organ music to create a Christian home, nor do you need to waft around the place with what Adrian Plass records in his *Sacred Diary* as the look of someone who has passed 'A' levels in ecstasy! Your home may have the lived-in look, but God wants the added impression that he lives there too.

## Housewife or homemaker?

How many times have you heard the familiar response to a question about a woman's occupation: 'I'm just a housewife'? That reply seems to indicate that running a home is a mundane job with no particular significance for society as a whole. Yet that is a long way from how this vitally important role should be seen. The Americans definitely have one over on the British because they refuse to use the word 'housewife' (perhaps because it conjures up the negative image of a woman chained to a house). Instead they use the word 'homemaker'. This word conveys a positive image of someone who creates a home; not so much someone who maintains, rather a person who creates.

We read the following extract in a British national newspaper a few years ago. The piece was written by Marianne Dennison, who quite obviously had not enjoyed her initiation into running a home:

> Fresh from the honeymoon and confronted with a large and rambling Victorian house, I whizzed around like a whirling tornado, not so much cleaning as dementedly trying to figure out *how* to clean the monster. Not quite in the Hoover bracket I had to make do with brush and pan and the weight fell off me as I tried to make

the nest gleaming and cosy for when daddy-bird came home.

After several years of marriage and a few children later she reaches the conclusion:

> Now older and wiser and bearing the scars of a long battle I am truly the mistress and manager of the house, albeit also accountant, nurse, plumber, mother, sister, lover, whipping-boy, chef and guru. It's a job that requires versatility of a high order ... Why should we feel intimidated by those women who seek their fulfilment outside the home?

Probably Marianne Dennison's struggle for survival is one with which many women can easily identify. But it seems to us that if marriage is truly a partnership, then that co-operation has to be expressed in the practical day-to-day routine of running a home. There is a part for both a husband and a wife to play in building a home together.

Let's begin with the woman's role. Traditionally it has been accepted in many societies that 'a woman's place is in the home'. In the western world that concept has been challenged in recent decades, where women have risen to positions of leadership in a variety of spheres. In the United Kingdom, the political landscape of the 1980s was dominated by the country's first woman Prime Minister. When Margaret Thatcher was first elected, a rather brave press reporter asked her husband, Denis, 'Who wears the pants in your house?'

'I do,' he answered promptly. After a pause he added, 'And I wash and iron them as well!'

The advent of married women pursuing separate careers has contributed to the change in the social fabric of Britain. Some would argue that this is a bad thing because it means that family life has suffered. Others point to the many plus factors this has produced, not least for women themselves who have felt liberated from their confinement to the four walls of the house. As with any argument, there are various pros and cons to be evaluated.

One thing is certain for a married woman: if you decide, for a few years at least, to continue full-time employment as well as building your home, life certainly will not be dull! You will need special stamina to cope with these demanding responsibilities.

A different stage is encountered when a woman decides to leave work in order to start a family. For the next few years running a home and organizing a family constitute more than a full-time job. Some women find this time in their lives rewarding and fulfilling; others have found it to be a great black cloud of drudgery and boredom.

A significant number of women choose to take the relatively short break of maternity leave and then resume work again. As with most things in life, this has advantages and disadvantages, but all who have chosen this particular route seem to agree that it takes skill and energy to operate smoothly.

A third stage in a married woman's life is the period when she possibly decides to go back to work on either a full-time or part-time basis. There are women who face this choice and decide not to work; others find it a welcome restoration of independence.

It seems to us there is an important ingredient which can make an enormous difference to the way you, as a woman, cope with your changing responsibilities. It is *attitude;* your attitude to your role as a wife, mother and homemaker will make all the difference to the way you tackle the job.

We can illustrate this from our own experience. Before our first son, Chris, was born, Ruth held down a highly responsible job. She had worked hard for her professional qualifications and had always felt totally fulfilled in her work. She loved motherhood and for a few years was absorbed in being a mum and minister's wife. By the time our third son, Jonathan, was born, Ruth was finding it more difficult to maintain her glow of enthusiasm. She found there were days when she longed to be free of demands, to pursue her own desires and to use her professional skills once more. It was at this time that Ruth underwent what she looks back on as a profound spiritual experience. Over a period of time, God began to show her that being a mum and housewife was not a job but a calling. At times, it might not be what she would choose to do. But the fact was that God had called her to do this task for a period of time. Ruth found that as she grasped this concept her attitude changed. God had called her to a vitally important role: to nurture and care for the four young lives that have been entrusted to our care for a few brief years; to provide a home for Ian which will be a haven; to support and provide back-up for his ministry. Ruth often describes this task by saying, 'My ministry is to enable Ian to keep functioning in his ministry.'

In short, the transformation that Ruth experienced came when God changed her attitude. She considered her role not just as a job to do, but as a calling from God.

The story is told of a man visiting the site where St Paul's Cathedral in London was being built. Inspecting the project, he asked a workman what job he was doing. 'I'm laying bricks,' the reply came.

He asked a second workman, who replied, 'I'm building a wall.'

He approached a third man, whose response was totally different: 'I'm helping Sir Christopher Wren construct the finest place of worship the world has ever seen!'

A positive attitude affects not only the way you look at your work but also the way you tackle it.

It is worth reminding ourselves, from time to time, why we are doing what we are doing. For the first few months of marriage, cleaning, shopping and even washing can be exciting. But when the enthusiasm starts to fade, remember who you are doing it for.

*For God.* The Bible teaches: 'Whatever you do, whether in

word or deed, do it all in the name of the Lord Jesus, giving thanks to God the Father through him' (Col. 3:17). With this in mind, work becomes worship.

*For your husband.* When you have time, read slowly and thoughtfully through Proverbs 31:10–31. The New International Version entitles this section, 'The Wife of Noble Character'. The passage teaches what a homemaker is meant to be, and it says of the wife's attitude to her husband: 'She brings him good, not harm, all the days of her life' (Pr. 31:12). Creating a home that is a haven for you both is a fulfilment of God's pattern for marriage.

*For your children.* If you feel frustrated at the mess your husband makes around the house you will soon discover that children can do it even more quickly! They seem to have a special ability to start untidying things before you have finished tidying them. But the environment you create for your children will have an influence on the whole of their lives. If your house is a constant mess, your children (plus you and your husband) will reflect that. If you treat it more like a museum of precious items of china, then your family will grow up expecting the attendant to shout at them every time they so much as breathe on a display cabinet!

*For your witness.* Many Christian women who are confined to the home discover that the home is a natural place for sharing their faith. Friends who come in and out will discover something about your faith from your home. A spotless house, lavishly furnished, is not what you need in order to convey the idea of a good Christian home. Practise the presence of Jesus, and even with the ironing half-done, children's toys strewn across the floor, and the baby throwing food at the cat, people will sense the difference that he makes in your lives. (Jesus, that is, not the cat!)

*For yourself.* Have you noticed that when you really want to do something it never seems like hard work? This brings us back to the whole business of our attitude affecting the way in which we tackle responsibilities. Taking a pride in your home is on the same level as taking a pride in your appearance. Of course, it is possible to become obsessed about both of these things. But with a balanced attitude it is right to spend time and energy creating a home that is a reflection of your taste and skills.

There will be times when ironing the same batch of shirts that you have ironed for months really gets to you. There will be days when you will feel like running away from home and leaving the family to fend for themselves. These are thoroughly normal reactions that every wife faces at times. But with God's help and a positive attitude, you will be able to see your responsibilities as a homemaker as they really are – a ministry.

## Leader or lodger?

A young couple set off on their honeymoon. When they arrived at the hotel where they were due to be staying for the fortnight, the young bride was overcome with embarrassment. Sitting in their car outside the hotel she told her husband that she couldn't face people knowing they were newly-weds and staring at them all the time. 'Can't we just pretend we've really been married for years?' she pleaded tearfully. 'OK,' her husband replied thoughtfully, 'But can you manage to carry four suitcases all by yourself?'

Point taken – we hope! Marriage is a partnership and we want to consider at this point the part that a husband has to play in building a Christian home. We are all products of our backgrounds. It may be that when you were a child your father did nothing to help in the house. He just expected to be waited on hand and foot as he presided as lord and master of all that he surveyed. Unfortunately, we learn a lot of wrong lessons from bad examples.

First of all, as a man you need to accept that there is

nothing 'non-macho' about washing up, ironing, cooking or changing a baby's nappy. Picking up a tea-towel will not challenge your virility! Second, in a true partnership both members of the team need to pull their weight. In the early years of marriage your wife will face many demands and if you leave every job around the house for her to tackle she will be worn out. The third reason for a husband to get involved in helping to run the home is, to our minds, the most powerful. Love is expressed by actions. Serving one another is the mark of a mature marriage. Your cooking may not be a patch on your wife's and she may be able to tackle the ironing in half the time it takes you. That is not the point. By volunteering to do these things you demonstrate love in a practical way.

Being a leader in your home does not mean sitting in an armchair issuing orders. Do you recall the example of true leadership which Jesus set? Servanthood. Remind yourself of his words which explained his example: 'Whoever wants to become great among you must be your servant, and whoever wants to be first must be your slave – just as the Son of Man did not come to be served, but to serve, and to give his life as a ransom for many' (Mt. 20:26–28).

To be an effective leader in your home, both as a husband and as a father, means being a servant. Here are some of the ways in which that can be put into practice.

*Helping hands.* Be prepared to cook a meal, help with the housework or look after the children. Don't wait to be asked, but make the offer loud and often. You may find, like a good number of men, that cooking is a very rewarding hobby.

*Spend time at home.* Your job may take you out of your house for many hours each week. Leisure-time activities will add more time away from home. But make certain that you learn to enjoy your home and make a contribution to the way it is run. Some men use their home as though they were lodgers, and that never builds a strong marriage.

*Don't take your partner for granted.* If you can learn to say 'thank you' and make appreciative comments, your wife will know that you are not taking her for granted. If you are full of criticism when dinner is a few minutes late, you may end up with it in your lap! Kind words are very important, and giving a bunch of flowers or box of chocolates will also help you to express your appreciation of your wife as a homemaker.

*Jobs around the house.* Some wives express great frustration at their husband's inability to tackle running repairs or handyman's jobs around the home. To be fair, not all men feel they are any good at fixing pelmets or mending leaking taps. Sometimes their wives are more skilled in these areas than they are. But when you constantly put off doing a job, the message that you communicate by your inaction is, 'I don't really care. I've got more important things to do.' That may not be the message you want to transmit, but that is exactly how it is received. The way you tackle your responsibilities helps your partner in the way she faces hers. Learn not to put off until tomorrow what you can do today.

We mentioned earlier that a home is a reflection of the personalities of the people who live there. It may be worth taking just a few minutes to look around your home to see what sort of picture you are creating. For better or worse, there is part of both of you in what you see. Perhaps some of it can be improved or tidied up a bit, but, as we have said before, marriage is a process of learning and growing together.

## Money matters

We have touched on finances already, but in the preparation and writing of this book we were taken by surprise at the number of couples who expressed the need for help in this area. Quite a few identified money matters as one of the biggest struggles of adjustment in their early years of marriage. We have to confess right away that we are not experts in this field by any stretch of the imagination. We have always found money matters a struggle in our marriage, and in our ignorance we were convinced our pressures were unique. This emphasizes, once again, the importance of being open with other Christians we can trust. By sharing our own weaknesses we can learn from others who have fought, and won, the same battles.

From our own financial ups and downs we have learned several principles that we now cling on to as to a life raft on a stormy sea.

## Get your giving right

If you are honouring God in your giving, then you can rest in the fact that he will honour you. We have learned that if you wait until you can afford it before you give, then you will never start to give. Make a determined decision at the beginning of married life that you intend to honour God through giving. Determine together how much of your income you are going to set aside for this purpose and where you believe God wants it directed. We have made this our number-one principle because we have learned the hard way that unless God comes first in our lives everything else is out of perspective.

## Work out a system

As with most things in life, money works best when it is organized. Between the two of you, work out a system that means you can plan how your income is used. For example, once you have sorted out your giving to the Lord you will have an amount left from which bills, housekeeping and other living expenses have to be met. Then there is the question of saving to be considered, especially when you are newly married and perhaps working towards a deposit on a house or furnishing your home.

All of the major banks operate various schemes to help you to budget your income. The local council-tax office, the gas and electricity companies and other services have plans whereby you can spread your total annual bills over equal monthly payments. These can make financial planning much easier.

Some couples have found it best to work to a formula or pattern. One we came across is called the 10–80–10 system. It simply means that 10% is the tithe (or tenth) that is taken off your salary for God's work, while 80% is the portion of your income that you live on. All your living expenses must be met from this portion. The final 10% is the amount you put on one side for savings each month.

For a couple with a total net income each month of £1,500 this would work out as follows:

> Giving to God: £150
> For savings account: £150
> Left to live on: £1,200

Working a system such as this, you are always living within your means. This is an area where couples run into difficulties because they spend all they earn and then find themselves with additional expenses they cannot meet from their income.

### Appoint a 'manager'

Whatever you decide about maintaining separate bank accounts or transferring to a joint account, it would be helpful if one of you took on the job of managing your accounts. (Personally, we strongly advocate joint finances because it demonstrates the partnership principle of a marriage relationship.) It may be that one of you is the natural choice for this job because you find figure work easy, or for some other reason. We have found that it is a job that one partner may tackle for a few years, and then, as circumstances change, the other partner may have more time to give to the matter of money management.

The appointment of one of you in this role means that things are not allowed to drift. One of you takes the responsibility of keeping a constant eye on income and expenditure.

## Discuss finances regularly

Although one partner may act as manager, you both need to sit down regularly and discuss financial affairs. We recommend that you create a routine when, say, one evening a month is used to discuss how you are spending your money. As most couples will tell you (if they are honest), discussions about money can easily develop into arguments. That does not mean we should avoid the discussions, but rather we need to learn to talk to each other with kindness and patience.

Most couples find the early years of marriage a tough struggle financially. A low income and rising bills can quickly produce sleepless nights and frayed tempers. Learn to pray and discuss things together and you will go a long way to getting a firm grip on financial affairs. When you discuss money matters, you need to agree such things as how much money it is reasonable to spend on housekeeping, what your priorities are for spending over the next few months and if there are ways in which you can cut down on some of the household bills. In short, it is a regular chance to communicate with each other about how you both use the resources God has entrusted to you.

One final word of caution. We firmly believe that it is wrong for one partner to embark on major expenditure without clearing it with the other. We are not talking about surprise birthday presents, but underlining the point that *interdependence* means what it says, especially in the area of finances.

## Watch your credit limits

The age of the little plastic card has ushered in many advantages and not a few dangers as well. A minister friend of ours recently conducted an informal, confidential survey among couples in his church to discover how many of them owed money through credit cards or hire-purchase agreements. He was stunned at the results. He began to teach and counsel in this whole area of borrowing because he was alarmed to discover so many couples who were struggling to repay large debts they had incurred through bad financial planning.

In today's world (at least in the western part of it), twenty-five-year mortgages and hire-purchase agreements have become part of normal everyday life. But as in so many areas we need to ensure that the world does not squeeze us into its own mould. Lending money is big business and we need to be aware of that. The temptation to over-borrow is always in front of us. Newspapers and direct-mail advertisements urge us to buy now and pay later, and we need to filter these invitations carefully.

Credit cards have the ability to make us spend without thinking; and, as any financial expert will tell you, for long-term borrowing they are very expensive. You would be better off applying for a loan from your bank if you wanted to borrow some money for a year or more, because the interest rate may well be lower.

One major credit-card company used to claim in their advertising that they 'take the waiting out of wanting'. But perhaps a little more waiting would help you to discover whether a particular 'want' is a genuine need.

If you find money matters a constant struggle, then why not look for some helpful advice? Your bank could be a good place to start, or you may know a couple older than yourselves who have worked through the tough parts of the early years. Their experience could be a means of help to you as you get to grips with money management.

## Planning your time

'I don't know where the week has gone.'

'We hardly have time to say "good morning" to each other!'

'Our weekends are busier than when we're at work.'

Do these comments sound familiar? If so, watch out. The chances are you are at overload in your allocation of time. We have already discussed in chapter 4, 'We don't talk any more', the value of planning time to spend together and especially the need for an 'oasis' to be created at regular intervals.

Time is like money. If you fail to plan how to spend it you will waste it. In establishing a home together you need to develop a pattern that suits your working hours and your personalities. Create time each day to pray and talk together. Make a regular date each week when you can spend uninterrupted time alone. Take opportunities during the year for special days out. In other words, plan your time together. Some couples have found it useful to keep a desk diary in a prominent place, where they can scribble in various reminders, such as which day one will be working late at the office or the night when the house-group leaders are due to meet. Try to include among the appointments an evening together or time to discuss next year's holiday plans. Whatever system you adopt for organizing your joint lives, we think you will agree that somewhere along the line, time together has to be planned; it won't just happen.

We found this particularly difficult when our children reached the age when they began to go to bed at a later hour. Evenings had been a time when we could sit down and discuss things, or simply enjoy being together. Suddenly the system had to alter to adapt to the changing needs of the family. We discovered the need to plan and use our time together even more carefully than before. We had to learn to use time during the day when the children were at school, or simply to make a clear rule that during an evening mum and dad needed to sit down and talk and (except in a dire emergency) there were to be no interruptions for half an hour.

Small issues become larger problems the longer they are

left. Planning regular times to talk can help you to keep those issues down to size.

## A place for others

Creating a home can be a very rewarding experience, particularly as you see everything gradually taking shape. It is fulfilling to see your hard work achieving something as the wallpaper, carpets and furnishings begin to transform the rooms. But if that is as far as it goes, it becomes a very self-centred experience. Your home is meant to be a haven, a place where you can be yourself and find refreshment; but it is more than this. It is meant to be a place for others too. Allowing others to enjoy the gift that God has entrusted to you is a demonstration of Christian love.

A few years ago we were speaking at a Christian conference in Britain. During the course of one of the teaching seminars, we posed the important question: 'Have you ever given your home back to God?' Later that day we met several young couples who said they had found the seminar helpful. They told us that a group of them had met together following the session to pray. 'We had a remarkable time,' one of the husbands told us. 'We just named before God things such as our houses, cars, and furniture and handed it all back to him!' The enthusiastic group discovered that day the joy that comes when you learn to give back to God what he has given to you, and when you allow him to use what he has entrusted to you.

In all the excitement of building your own home we would urge you not to miss out on the wonderful dimension of letting others share it with you. Hospitality is a spiritual gift; it is not particularly spectacular but it is still greatly needed and valued. Take a look around your church and you will soon discover a crowd of people who would value some friendship and a good meal: students living away from home, single people, the elderly or bereaved. Please don't forget couples with small children either.

It is a good thing to develop the habit of entertaining non-Christian friends regularly at home. One of the first contacts people have with the Christian faith is within the four walls of a home. If you happen to use your house for a home Bible study group, then why not hold an open meeting several times a year? The idea would be that each group member brings along a non-Christian friend for a less formal evening with a supper, and perhaps a guest speaker or an evangelistic video.

We look back with real gratitude to several couples who opened their homes to us when we were single. From our vantage-point now, as parents, we realize what a sacrifice this was. But it was an investment of time in our lives for which we will always be grateful.

We like to use several different pictures to think of our home: it is *a painting* because it embodies a reflection of our personalities; it is a *castle* where we can withdraw from the world and find safety and security; it is a *garden* where others can appreciate the scenery and enjoy eating the fruit; it is a *temple* because God, by his Spirit, lives in the people who live there. We freely admit that there are times when it is more like a fairground, a battlefield, or even a railway station. But as with most things in life, aspiring and striving towards the goal are half the fun.

God has given you your home; enjoy it – and use it.

# CHAPTER EIGHT

# STARTING A
## FAMILY

When the time arrives and you decide together to start a family, hold your breath. You are about to embark upon the most demanding yet potentially exhilarating phase of married life. When a couple become a family it is more than just a case of another mouth to feed. You are starting a whole new chapter of your relationship together. When, in the goodness of God, you hold that warm bundle of flesh in your arms for the first time, you will probably feel a sense of awe: first, because you are holding a living being born out of your love for each other, and second, because you begin to realize the incredible potential locked up in that tiny package of life.

We came across the following words of a man by the name of E. T. Sullivan. It helped us to interpret something of the awesomeness that new parents sometimes feel.

> When God wants a great work done in the world or a great wrong righted, he goes about it in a very unusual way. He doesn't stir up his earthquakes or send forth his thunderbolts. Instead, he has a helpless baby born, perhaps in a simple home and of some obscure mother. And then God puts the idea into the mother's heart, and she puts it into the baby's mind. And then God waits.
>
> The greatest forces in the world are not the earthquakes and the thunderbolts. The greatest forces in the world are babies.

What, or more precisely who, determines whether a child becomes a Louis Pasteur or a Joseph Stalin, a Mother Teresa or an Adolf Hitler? Without a doubt, parenting and family life play an enormous part in the development of a child, mentally, emotionally, physically and spiritually.

When family life is strong then society is strong. What we are doing (or not doing) in the home has repercussions for the wider world.

In this chapter we are considering how we can tackle the transition from being a couple to becoming a family. We are covering the period of time between deciding to start a family to the first months after the baby has been born. In other words, we are dealing with the foundations for building a family. There are plenty of books on family life and bringing up children which will be of help to you, but we seek only to deal with the beginnings.

## Deciding to start a family

We have already mentioned in chapter 6, 'Loving and learning', the need to discuss your attitudes about starting a family as you prepare for marriage. We have met several couples who have taken the view that to plan for a child is either too mechanical or totally unspiritual. Sometimes there are special circumstances which cause a newly married couple to decide against any form of family planning, thereby making it more likely that a child will be born early in the relationship. Also, some couples dispense with contraceptive methods because of strongly held religious views. But we believe that experience proves that it is wise for a couple to enjoy the benefits of medical science and specifically plan towards the right time to start a family.

Expert opinion suggests that babies have a better start in life if they have:

- parents who aren't too young
- parents who are happily married
- parents who have a good enough home
- parents who know that a baby is hard work

- parents who are ready to enjoy family life
- parents who know how important a baby's needs are

Making the decision to start a family brings us back to a word which seems to crop up in every chapter of this book: *communication*. Good communication plays an important part in the different aspects of marriage. As partners you need to agree together about the timing of the birth of your first child, you need to listen to each other's opinion and pray through the issue together. Here are some of the key questions that will help you to talk over your feelings together.

*Do we have a secure relationship?* Have you matured as a couple and are you establishing a balanced, loving marriage? Are you working through some of the adjustments that you have both had to make in the early years of marriage? Is your love for each other growing?

*Is our living accommodation adequate and secure?* Do you have a large enough home to cope with the arrival of a baby and are you securely settled there for the foreseeable future? If not, do you have the financial resources to move to a larger home?

*Are we coping financially?* Have you thought through the implications of losing a whole income if one of you stops work? Will you be able to manage on this reduced sum, bearing in mind the extra expenses involved in having a child? If you opt for maternity leave, have you sat down and worked out the financial implications? Have you discussed child-minding costs?

*Are we linked to a good local church?* Have you integrated as a couple into your church? Are you making real friendships within the church? Are you growing together in the spiritual dimension of your marriage?

*Are we prepared for the changes in our lifestyle and the extra demands a baby will make?* Are you realistically facing up to what it means to have a baby? Have you talked over some of the changes you will need to make in your lives? Are you both willing to make these adjustments?

*Have we talked and prayed the decision through together?* Do you believe you have given time to discuss things? Have you really heard what your partner is saying (and feeling) about having a baby? Are you including God in your plans, seeking his guidance by praying together?

Possibly you feel overwhelmed by looking at all these questions, having thought that starting a family was not such a complex business! But bringing a baby into the world is an important decision and you can't change your mind after six months if you find parenthood doesn't suit you. Think the issues through together and prepare the ground well for the transition from two to three.

It is also worth remembering several wrong reasons for having a baby:

- one partner pressurizes the other partner into a decision
- believing that having a baby can patch up a relationship that is cracking up
- pressure from parents or friends
- the attitude that says, 'I suppose it's about time we got round to it.'

We have heard of situations where one partner has tricked the other into a pregnancy by pretending to use contraceptive protection – hardly the best way to develop a relationship of trust.

As with all 'the best laid plans of mice and men', mistakes do happen, and that is not all bad. The writers of this book happen to be the products of unplanned pregnancies, and even if no-one else believes that 'mistakes' can be good, the two of us do! There are many couples who have seen the hand of God at work in their lives when a child has been conceived unexpectedly, and not many of us would want to live in a world of neat and predictable events. God is sovereign, so you can trust him with the details of your family life.

Once you have both decided to try to start a family there are several things to remember. First, relax and be patient; give yourselves time to conceive. If you think about it, there are a limited number of days in each month when this is physically possible, so if several months pass without any evidence that you have conceived it probably means nothing more than the fact that intercourse has not coincided with the most fertile time in the cycle. Second, see it as an exciting and enjoyable time in your lives. Enjoy sexual love to the full; learn to express your love in different ways. Be positive in your approach and don't suddenly become clinical in your love-making. Third, if after twelve months you have still not conceived, make an appointment to see either your doctor or the Family Planning Clinic. Seeking professional advice like this is quite usual and there is no need to expect them to do anything other than check out that you are not in need of specialized help. It is better to seek advice than simply allow matters to drag on.

## Preparing for the new arrival

Nine months can seem a very long time when you are pregnant. The time from the confirmation of your pregnancy (which, of course, is less than nine months) until the happy event can sometimes be a frustrating time of waiting. This preparation period, we believe, is part of God's plan for us as human beings because he knows that the arrival of a baby means that adjustments have to be made in our lives and we need time for these to take place. If a baby could be planned today and arrive in the middle of next week you simply would not have enough time to get ready.

To begin with there are *practical preparations* that need to be made. These range from purchasing what sometimes may seem like a warehouse-full of equipment to preparing a bedroom for the new arrival. The glossy brochures may suggest that you need the latest brand-new baby products, but you will probably find that a chat with a couple who already have a baby will help you work out what you can get by without. Most antenatal clinics provide booklets and leaflets packed with helpful advice for parents-to-be. We have discovered that the second-hand maternity market is a booming industry, as a glance through the small ads in your local newspaper will bear out. If you are operating on a tight budget this is one way to cut costs considerably and you can often pick up some good bargains in excellent condition.

You might find it useful to make a list of things you need to purchase and preparations that need to be made. In our own experience of four pregnancies, Ian discovered what he called Ruth's 'nest-building phase' when the planning for the new arrival dominated almost every moment of her daylight hours. This is an important factor in preparing for the birth of your baby and can be a special help to you both in adjusting to the prospect of parenthood.

It is also good to use this time to *prepare yourselves* by taking extra time to talk together and look forward to the birth of your baby. We have found it helpful to create some special times together. For example, if it is at all possible, the opportunity of a good, relaxing holiday with just the two of you will give you the physical rest you both need. After all, it will probably be quite a few years before you will be able to enjoy each other's company in quite the same way again.

If your child is going to be born into an atmosphere of love then you need to spend time building up the stock cupboard. Pregnancy poses some practical problems when it comes to love-making, but it can be fun learning to overcome them together.

Many couples find this preparation period a time when they can talk about their future plans and dreams. Look ahead to the future. You are leaving BC (Before Children) for AD (After Delivery). Share what you want to build together as a family. There is one word of caution that we would inject at this point:

don't let your excitement isolate you from friends and family. Although the main thing dominating your horizon at this time is the birth of your baby, there are other important things happening in the world as well. In the future you will value the support and help of family and friends, so don't allow yourselves to become isolated.

Pregnancy is an exciting time for grandparents-to-be as well, and although overbearing interference is not a helpful thing, it is good to allow them to share in the exciting build-up to the birth of your baby.

Inevitably you will be using these months to *prepare for the actual birth*. The level of antenatal and postnatal care in western countries is very high indeed, and increasingly that care is seen to include helping the prospective parents to prepare for this special experience. Through her regular visits to the antenatal clinic a woman will be given all sorts of information about what to expect, and often a series of preparation classes for both partners will be offered. We strongly recommend that you *both* seize every opportunity that is given to help you in this respect. For example, a visit to the maternity unit of the hospital (which is often included in the preparations for couples) is a great help in removing some of the mystique that surrounds childbirth, and it is not half as off-putting as you may expect. If you have questions, no matter how trivial they may seem to you, make sure that you ask them when you visit the clinic or special classes.

The National Childbirth Trust run a series of five or six antenatal classes, covering pregnancy, birth and early parenthood. Their head office is mentioned in the 'Useful addresses' section at the back of this book, but there are plenty of local groups, which should be listed in your local telephone directory.

Our own experience has been that the more you can learn before the event, the better prepared you will be when it happens. Things such as knowing what to have ready in your suitcase, and learning to discover the signs that you really are in labour, go a long way to calming your nerves as the great day approaches.

One thing that we encourage every couple to discuss is whether or not the husband should be present for the actual birth. Most hospitals positively encourage husbands to be actively involved in the various stages of pregnancy, including being present in the delivery room when 'D day' arrives. Couples take different views as to whether this is a good idea or not. You need to decide what is right for *you*, and not worry about what anyone else may think. We approached this decision in our own lives with mixed feelings, but decided that as we had been together when the baby was conceived, we might as well stay together to see it all through!

Personally, we are glad that Ian was present at the birth of all of our children, and we look back on those experiences as among the most special in our lives. Other matters such as methods of natural childbirth and the pros and cons of home delivery can be raised when you visit the antenatal clinic. Don't be put off by the uniforms and apparent officialdom. You have the right to discuss these things and most people engaged in the medical profession are dedicated and caring individuals.

Preparing for the arrival of your baby can be a fulfilling time. Despite the old wives' tales about labour and the sometimes less-than-helpful comments of friends about the traumas of teething babies and broken nights, we want to assure you that becoming parents is a wonderful experience. Naturally, you will find some adjustments more difficult than others, but we urge you not to let anyone rob you of the joy and special blessing of becoming a mum and dad.

## Things a new dad needs to know

You may be surprised that we have placed this section ahead of the next, 'Things a new mum needs to know', but our decision is deliberate. During pregnancy, childbirth and the first months of your baby's life, a great deal of attention is paid to your wife, and rightly so. There is the danger that, as a husband, you can simply feel like a spectator. Yet you have an important part to fulfil in the transition from being a couple to becoming a family.

As with all new experiences, learning to be a father takes time and you will probably learn more through making mistakes than anything else. Here are some of the things that you may possibly encounter during the first few months of being a dad.

### Don't be surprised if you feel threatened

Many new fathers have expressed the feeling of being 'left out' when the baby is born. The focus of everyone's attention becomes the baby and the woman who produced him or her. Your wife's time and attention will temporarily be concentrated on the little life that is dependent on her. She may at times seem totally preoccupied with the baby, so much so that the fact that baby brought his wind up in record time today may become the main item of news when you come home after a hard day at work. This is where the storehouse supply of love becomes important; draw on yesterday's experience of your wife's love for you to help you face the fact that for the moment, someone else is the centre of her attention.

### Expect your routine to change

You will quickly discover that babies do not work nine-till-five days (or nights), but they have their own quite interesting routine. Also, your wife will be playing hostess to a succession of visitors ranging from midwives and doctors through to friends and family. You may have been used to your meal being on the table at the same time each evening but the change in your wife's routine inevitably produces a change in yours. This is when patience and understanding are needed. Also, you need to be willing to tackle some of the tasks your wife usually does. Your routine will soon adapt and, believe it or not, you will soon be able to move round the hallway without stepping over prams and carrycots.

## In your sexual relationship
### things will be different, for a time

Your wife has to adjust to the physical demands of having a baby. Her body needs time to heal and return to normal. In addition, there are changes in her hormones at this time, all connected with childbirth and perhaps breastfeeding. You need to understand this, be patient and recognize that it is a phase that will pass. Your partner's inability to enjoy full inter-course does not mean that she has no need of physical love. Cuddling, kissing and affectionate words will go a long way to helping her to adjust. A soothing massage may be the very thing she needs and is one way you can express your care for her.

As her body adjusts back to its usual shape, your wife will need reassurance about her appearance. Be very careful about personal comments, even in a teasing manner, because this is a time when she needs all the encouragement she can get.

The length of time it takes for you to get back into a regular sexual relationship varies greatly, but keep up the actions of affection and let your wife decide when she feels able to try full intercourse. If after a few months she is finding things difficult (either physically or mentally) then we recommend you seek medical advice.

One word of encouragement for you both is that this interruption in your usual enjoyment of love-making is only for a short time. Most couples find that it is not long, probably only a few weeks, before things are back to normal.

Be prepared for changes in your wife's emotions. Having a baby is the biggest event in a woman's life; every part of her being is involved in carrying, delivering and nurturing your child. You will have noticed during pregnancy that your wife underwent various changes emotionally as well as physically. These changes continue for a short time after the baby has been born. There is no need to think that your wife is having a nervous breakdown just because she bursts into tears more often or finds things difficult to cope with. If you are prepared for these changes you will be able to give her the stability and love she needs at this time.

## At times you will feel like a spare part

Some husbands have found that after the birth of the baby they feel quite useless. Your wife's responsibilities are clearly defined, but what exactly is a new dad supposed to *do?* This can be compounded by the presence of well-meaning relatives who seem to muscle in and take over. Perhaps mother-in-law appears on the scene and you feel pushed to the sidelines and, although you appreciate her kind thought, you can sometimes feel like a stranger in your own home.

There is no short answer to this feeling other than to remember that this is a phase most couples work through. It will not last for ever, and you will soon be able to feel 'at home' again at home.

## Take responsibility

If you try to help all you can, the adjustment process will be much easier to handle and you will feel less of a spare part. Perhaps your wife is preoccupied with the baby, but that probably means there are jobs that she would usually tackle which you can take on.

## Remember: every baby is different,
### and so are their mums

Earlier in the book we warned of the danger of comparing yourselves with other couples, because each marriage is unique. The same principle applies to motherhood and babies. For example, if you tell your wife, 'Julie's baby sleeps right through the night and she has to wake him in the morning,' or 'I don't know why you look so depressed. My sister went wind-surfing the weekend after her youngest was born,' we suggest that you practise ducking to avoid flying objects!

Comparisons are unfair and can be unkind. This is your wife's first try at being a mother; give her the chance to do it her own way. As for 'textbook babies', in our experience either they don't exist or they can't read.

## Don't panic!

Some friends shared with us their first few traumatic weeks as new parents. Their baby slept in their bedroom and as a result they spent most nights wide awake listening for every little grunt or squeak. When things were quiet they would leap out of bed to make sure their child was still breathing. Years later they could laugh together about it, but at the time they were living in a constant state of tension.

Your major contribution as a husband and a father at this new stage in your marriage is to provide stability. Your wife and child want to rest in the security that you can give them. In turn, you need to be leaning on God in a greater way than before in your life. As you face anxieties, adjustments and decisions, ask God to make his peace your peace.

Fatherhood grows on you. If you can recall the experience of starting a new job you will find some helpful parallels in learning to cope with fatherhood. On your first day you probably felt a little strange as you were introduced, and it took several weeks to settle into the job and remember everyone's name. Possibly it was quite a few months before you felt you had thoroughly mastered everything you were being asked to do. Like a favourite armchair, the job began to fit your shape.

Fatherhood is like that. It takes time, practice and not a few mistakes. The more you tense up and try to be a father, the less progress you will make. Enlist God's help and daily commit yourself, your wife and child to his care. Ask him for the wisdom you need to be an effective father; he is bound not to turn you down (see Jas. 1:5).

# Things a new mum needs to know

Some women find that motherhood comes naturally to them, but others find it quite a struggle to come to terms with the new responsibilities that a baby brings. Probably the most important thing you need to hold on to at this time in your life is the need to be yourself. Magazines and books give all sorts of patterns for the ideal 'young mum', but you need to discover for yourself how best to adjust to this new stage in your life. Here are a few guidelines to help you to design your own blueprint for motherhood.

## Be prepared for the feeling of anticlimax

It is a well-attested fact that all women hit a 'blues' patch within a few days of giving birth, usually around the tenth day after delivery. Be prepared for that to happen and don't let yourself become over-anxious about your emotional response. You have just come through an enormous physical experience that has affected every part of your body, mind and emotions, and you should expect a reaction as a result.

For a few women the feelings of depression can be more acute, and if these persist you need to tell your doctor or midwife. Postnatal depression takes a variety of forms and can usually be treated effectively. There is no reason to think that you are an unspiritual, weak Christian if this should affect you in one form or another. Plenty of committed Christian women have been through the same experience and have discovered God's help and healing.

## Don't try to be Superwoman

Women respond to having a baby in different ways. Some find themselves feeling utterly lethargic and unable to get back into the routine of life. Others respond by immediately throwing themselves into everything with the determination to prove that they can cope. Subconsciously they can be trying to demonstrate to the world how good they are at adjusting to motherhood.

The truth is that you do not have to prove yourself to anyone. Some jobs will be left undone and there will be a break in your usual routine of running the home, so tell yourself you have nothing to prove. Taking each day at a time will help you to pace yourself as you adjust to a new pattern of living.

## Love and include your husband

If you have not done so already, we suggest you read through the previous section, 'Things a new dad needs to know'. From reading that it will be apparent, we hope, that your husband is undergoing his own adjustments to the changes in your lives. He needs to be reassured of your love for him and you can do this in a variety of ways. Include him in the times of feeding and bathing the baby. Let him hold your child and express your delight in seeing him do that. It can be very frustrating for a woman to stand back and watch a man struggling to change a baby's nappy, but a simple thing like that (if he has got the courage!) can be a real boost to his confidence.

When it comes to the physical side of your relationship, remember that although full sexual intercourse will be out of the question for a short time, he still has needs in this area. Reach out to him with affection and stimulate and satisfy him by cuddling and touching. Although you may feel tired try to give him time to express his feelings at this new phase in your lives together.

A number of women find the help of family and friends invaluable during the first few weeks after the baby's arrival. Without losing this input, you need to recognize it is easy for your husband to feel isolated, so do all you can to include him.

## Organize your time

Your life will revolve around the waking, sleeping and feeding times of the new baby. This will place extra demands on you and it is essential that you work out a system of some sort to help you cope. For example, make a list of priority jobs you can tackle during the times baby is asleep. Having a list will save you from the frustration of puzzling about what to do next. At times you need to use the periods when baby is asleep to put your feet up and enjoy a rest yourself. There is no need to feel the slightest bit guilty about this. It is not a case of self-indulgence but rather self-preservation.

You can find ways to use feeding times constructively as well. They can be a time for looking ahead and planning, or spending some minutes reading the Bible and praying. Some women have found cassettes of worship music or teaching ministry a great help at such times. These suggestions are not meant to rob you of the delight of nursing your baby, which can be a precious experience all by itself.

## Be aware of changes in your emotions

Looking after a new baby makes many demands on you. As well as the changes taking place in the hormones in your body, there is the constant battle with tiredness associated with coping with a new experience. This can lead to changes in your emotions and sometimes these can be quite dramatic. For example, you may find yourself near to tears at times, or on other occasions short-tempered. The most trivial incident can become a major crisis because of this emotional roller-coaster you seem to be riding.

Give yourself time to adjust, and make sure you get the amount of rest you need. If, at times, there are outbursts, apologize and put things right. This helps to clear the air and reassures those who are close to you that you do really love them after all.

## Be aware of 'baby-mindedness'

One of the dangers of becoming a new mum is that your whole life is dominated by this tiny human being. For a time your universe will revolve around this newcomer who rules your world from the pram. But remember, in the real world life still goes on. Your husband, family and friends are interested in how your baby is growing but remember to ask them what is happening in their lives.

It can be a frustrating experience to meet a woman who has no conversation apart from her baby. Other people will be more willing to share your excitement if you remember to show an interest in them as well.

## Creating a happy, loving home is your priority

Try not to turn your house into an extension of Mothercare. Babies do need a lot of extra bits and pieces of special equipment, but if you are not careful this can easily become an obsession. Often a group of young mums in a community will arrange a 'swap and share' scheme whereby carrycots, potties, stairguards and highchairs can be passed on from one to another. Not only does that make good economic sense, but it helps to prevent your home becoming cluttered with things you will not necessarily need all at one time – unless of course you have a large loft!

Not everything 'happens naturally'. Contrary to information in books and expert opinions, you will soon discover that your child is unique. For most mums things do not always 'happen naturally'. Often it is a case of trial and error, working by the process of elimination as you seek to care for your baby as an individual. Some babies sleep better than others, some struggle with feeding, others adopt their own way of doing things. Regular visits to the postnatal clinic will help monitor your baby's progress and you can use these opportunities to ask questions and receive advice. It is always better to seek expert medical advice if you are worried than to rely on bits and pieces of information picked up through hearsay.

The home is the training-school for life, but thankfully it is not a school that God intends you to run all by yourself. The Bible has much to say on the subject of families and it tackles the responsibilities of fathers, mothers and children. We believe that one of the greatest needs in the West at this time, as well as in other parts of the world, is to see the establishment of families built according to God's pattern.

As you build your family life together you will face many issues, choices and decisions. It is good to know that God is committed to helping us. Parenthood is a process of learning as you go. We have found that we learn by our mistakes as much as anything else. The help and encouragement you can receive through prayer, the studying and application of the Bible in daily life, the friendship of other Christians and the support of a good local church are ways in which God demonstrates his commitment to us as families.

One of the greatest temptations parents face is to neglect their children. You can give a child everything from a material point of view, but if you fail to give discipline or time or love, then you are guilty of neglect. The most precious gift we can ever give to our children is *ourselves*. The Police Department in Houston, Texas, reflected something of this when they produced the following warning to parents:

### Twelve rules for raising delinquent children

1 Begin with infancy to give the child everything he [or she] wants. In this way he will grow up to believe that the world owes him a living.
2 When he picks up bad words, laugh at him. This will

make him think he is cute. It will also encourage him to pick up 'cuter' phrases later that will blow the top of your head off.

3   Never give him any spiritual training. Wait till he is 21, then let him 'decide for himself'.

4   Avoid the use of the word 'wrong' – it may develop a guilt complex. This will condition him to believe later, when he is arrested for stealing a car, that society is against him and he is being persecuted.

5   Pick up everything that he leaves lying around – books, shoes, clothing. Do everything for him so he will be experienced in throwing all responsibility on to others.

6   Let him read any printed matter that he can get his hands on. Be careful that the silverware and drinking glasses are sterilized, but let his mind feed on garbage.

7   Quarrel frequently in the presence of your children. In this way they will not be too shocked when the home is broken up later.

8   Give your child all the spending money he wants. Never let him earn his own. Why should he have things as tough as you had them?

9   Satisfy his every craving for food, drink and comfort. See that every sensual desire is gratified. Denial may lead to harmful frustration.

10  Take his side against teachers, neighbours and policemen. They are all prejudiced and against your child.

11  When he gets into real trouble, apologize for yourself by saying, 'I never could do anything with him.'

12  Prepare for a life of grief – you're going to have it.

That makes sobering reading, but over and above it, place the many scriptures that speak of giving our children love, security, discipline, instruction about God, a sense of responsibility towards others and the ability to develop true values and you will be well on the way to discovering the joys of parenthood.

Our prayer for ourselves, as well as for you, is that by building our family life according to God's pattern we might prove the truth of the proverb which says, 'Children's children are a crown to the aged, and parents are the pride of their children' (Pr. 17:6).

# YOU DON'T BRING ME FLOWERS

An elderly couple were celebrating their platinum wedding: seventy years of married bliss. An eager young radio reporter was sent to cover the story and did his best to try to make the old man (who was very deaf) understand his questions. 'Seventy years is a long time,' the reporter shouted in the old man's ear. 'Have you ever contemplated divorce during that time?' There were a few seconds of silence as the old boy toyed with the question in his mind, and then, with a decided twinkle in his eye, he responded, 'Divorce? No, I can't say I've ever thought of that. Mind you, I've considered murder several times!'

We believe that most married couples can enter into the spirit of that reply. Marriage can, on occasions, bring the worst parts of human nature to the surface.

The purpose of this book is to help us build the right foundations for marriage. After all, if the foundations are secure, the rest of the building is safe (see Mt. 7:24–27). But beyond the 'early years' we need to learn how to build wisely on the foundations that have been laid. Think for a moment about the words of the marriage ceremony and recall the vows that are exchanged:

> According to God's will, I call upon these persons here present to witness that I do take thee to be my lawful wedded wife/husband to have and to hold from this day forward, for better or worse, for richer or poorer, in sickness and in health, to love and to cherish, till we are parted by death, and to this end I give you my word.

There seems, in the words of the wedding service, a healthy realization that marriage is a patchwork quilt of experiences joined together. There are good times and bad, laughter as well as tears. We are being totally unrealistic if we fail to recognize this and prepare ourselves for it. Perhaps one of the reasons such a large proportion of marriages end in divorce is that couples have expectations that are too high. When problems occur they opt to take the quick way out instead of working through to a solution together. As we said in chapter 1, *marriage needs to be worked at.*

We recently read a moving story about commitment in marriage, which came from the pen of American author Fred Smith. He was eating a meal in a restaurant in Texas and noticed a young couple at the next table. He spotted that when the husband went to pay the bill his wife didn't get up to follow him. He continues: 'But then he came back and stood in front of her. She put her arms around his neck, and he lifted her up, revealing that she was wearing a full body brace. He lifted her out of her chair and backed through the front door to the pick-up truck with her hanging from his neck.

'As he gently put her in the truck, everyone in the restaurant watched. No-one said anything until a waitress remarked, almost reverently, "He took his vows seriously."'

That's commitment.

## The most important word in marriage

If you were asked to give the most important word in a marriage relationship, how would you reply? 'Love', 'sex', possibly 'happiness'? In fact, the most important word in marriage is *commitment.* There are times when love is strained, sex is boring and happiness hard to find. It is in times like these that commitment undergirds a relationship.

On your wedding day you made a solemn commitment

before God to each other. Every day since, you have faced the implications of working through those promises in the changing seasons of life. Sadly, people change and circumstances alter, sometimes resulting in the total breakdown of a marriage. We have been around too long to deny the fact that this does happen, even to Christian couples. Possibly as you read this book you look back with sadness on a failed marriage. The Christian gospel is one of hope, and we want to encourage you to realize that God is able to heal the past and deliver us from repeating mistakes, provided that we are willing to submit our lives to his guidance and control.

Commitment implies giving ourselves totally to someone or something, conveying the idea of dogged determination to keep going when things get tough. We have known times in our own marriage when we have needed to ask God to strengthen our commitment to each other, as well as to him. There have been times when we have had to hang on, not being certain that we would make it. God has been faithful in helping us through, and that is the experience of thousands of couples the world over.

We have also come to realize that there are specific things that *we* can do to strengthen that commitment and keep romance alive along the way. In the course of the year we are used to the changing seasons: winter, spring, summer and autumn. Each time of the year has a distinctive feel about it. Marriage passes through seasons as well: the early years, starting a family, coping with small children, then the teenage years, life with just the two of you again, and so on. For all the changes which these different phases may bring, some factors need to remain constant if our commitment to one another is to be real.

# Loving through the
## changing seasons

In order to face the changing seasons of married life with confidence, we have found that there are four important words that help us to express our commitment to each other:

- affirmation
- demonstration
- evaluation
- communication

These words are best explained in personal terms as we consider what an individual partner is seeking to express. *Affirmation* means that I love you and remain committed to you in the terms and sentiments of our marriage vows. *Demonstration* means that I will prove my love and commitment to you by my words, attitudes and actions. *Evaluation* means that I will play a full part in assessing my contribution to our marriage, with a willingness to work through areas of difficulty that my behaviour may cause at times. *Communication* means that I promise to communicate my feelings with honesty and love, and that I will listen to what you have to say with patience and understanding.

You will notice how often the words 'I' and 'my' occur. This puts the ball in the court where it belongs. Too often we expect our partner to change and we fail to realize our own responsibilities. We must begin with ourselves.

In order to understand the meaning of these four words, let us consider how they are worked out in the context of everyday life.

We are able to *affirm* our love and commitment in a variety of ways. It is a good thing regularly to remind your partner that you are glad that you married him or her. Another word for 'affirmation' is 'confirmation'. We confirm that our marriage vows are as important today as on the day we first made them. We know of some couples who, on a special occasion, such as a wedding anniversary, will replay the recording of their wedding service in order to remind themselves of the happy day. We have also shared in special thanksgiving services when a couple have renewed their vows in thanksgiving to God. Such times are a special rededication of our lives to each other and to the Lord. But you don't need a special anniversary to remind your partner of your commitment. One of the best ways we have discovered to keep love growing stronger is regularly to affirm our commitment to each other.

You can *demonstrate* your love for one another through words, attitudes and actions. Learn to say, 'I love you', without embarrassment, because those three words can, at times, heal a lot of differences. Buying a special present, writing a love letter or planning a surprise evening out are all ways in which we can demonstrate our love. The best antidote to taking each other for granted is to look for ways in which you can show your partner that he or she is special to you.

It is significant that when you ask most couples to pin-point a weak area in their relationship, the answer most often heard is, 'Taking each other for granted.' That is why the occasional impulsive act of gratitude is so valuable. Two friends of ours discovered this when the husband, who was away from home on a business trip, suddenly returned home unexpectedly early. He went to his wife's place of work and, using his spare set of car keys, deposited a large bouquet of flowers on the driver's seat. He hid in another part of the car park and watched her mystified reaction as she came to leave for home. He then trailed her home in his car before bringing her to a halt with a flash of his headlamps. After a very touching reunion on the kerbside, his tearful wife confessed that she thought she had an unknown admirer who had left the flowers for her!

We need constantly to *evaluate* our marriage, especially

when we face times of pressure or changes in circumstances. We have tried to emphasize throughout this book the need to give each other sufficient time for evaluation. The pace of life today means that unless you plan specific times to talk together, months will pass by without any meaningful opportunities to assess where your marriage is in need of some attention.

Holidays can often provide a chance to spend time talking things over together, although with the demands of a young family you may find a holiday more pressured than life at home! That is why we believe it is helpful for every couple to plan, every so often, to have some time on their own. Perhaps you can find someone willing to look after the children only for a day or evening at the most, rather than a complete weekend. But take the opportunity of time together to evaluate your marriage. That means more than just listing complaints about your partner. Learn to build each other up by expressing how grateful you are about certain things in one another that make your marriage strong. One practical exercise you may find helpful is for you both to draw up two lists, one headed 'Things I thank God for in my marriage' and the other 'Things I need God to help me with in my marriage'. When you have the opportunity for some quality time together, compare the lists you have both made. You could be in for an interesting time.

We have constantly returned to the need for a husband and wife to *communicate* well with each other. But for some couples, good communication is hampered because honest conversations always seem to end in blazing rows. Rather than face another argument, some couples prefer to let things slide in the desire for a quiet life. We have found that this is a shortsighted view. You may have an argument-free day today, but unless things are out in the open you could be storing up trouble for tomorrow.

Good communication means that you are willing to listen as well as to express your views. If we spent more time hearing what our partner is saying then the arguments would become less frequent. It seems to us that a good motto for any married couple is 'He who has ears, let him hear' (Mt. 11:15).

If you incorporate these four principles in your marriage you will be building well on a firm foundation. Affirmation, demonstration, evaluation and communication are all needed to help us face the changing seasons of married life.

## Keeping romance alive

Many couples have a favourite song or piece of music that has particular significance for them. Perhaps it is a song that was played on the night that they met, or a piece of music which brings to mind a special moment. Like most, we have our own musical memories. Barbra Streisand is a particular favourite for both of us, and one of her songs has always been a 'special'. It is one that reminds us how not to love. We have always found it a sad reminder of a marriage where the fire has gone out. The title is 'You Don't Bring Me Flowers'. It is a haunting duet in which a couple recount the ways in which they have both realized that their relationship has slowly died. The kind words and loving actions have fallen away like dead leaves. The poignancy of the song is that they both realize that something that once was so special is no more.

It may well be that the voices of Barbra Streisand and Neil Diamond have something to do with it, but we rarely hear that song without feeling a chill down our spines. There are few sights more tragic than a couple who have fallen out of love. In the same way, one of the most heartwarming sights is an elderly couple still obviously very much in love. The years seem to have welded them together rather than pulled them apart.

So what makes the difference? Or is marriage no more than a roulette wheel of fate where, if you are lucky, the right number and colour come up?

The issue is not so much *what* makes the difference as *who*. Your marriage is not, to change the analogy, a little life-raft bobbing around on the sea of fate. God initiated marriage and chooses to be intimately involved in it. A husband and a wife have their responsibilities too. But facing marriage on the basis that it is a trio rather than a duet removes fatalism or good luck from the scene.

'Happily ever after' is more than the stuff from which fairy tales are made. And for the couple who are committed to living God's way in their marriage, the doorway is opened to a lifetime of joy. Fulfilling the Maker's plans brings untold fulfilment which reaches beyond ourselves and affects the very roots of the society in which we live.

Our love for each other can become a means of touching our world with God's love. As we practise forgiveness, we show to the world God's forgiveness made possible through his Son, Jesus Christ. As we demonstrate commitment, we reveal something of God's commitment to men and women. As we build marriage and family life according to the Creator's pattern, we prove that his ways are best. As we practise hospitality, we provide a reminder of the welcome God gives to those who, in hearing the gospel of Jesus, choose to come home. In short, your marriage can be more than a selfish love affair from the script of a Hollywood movie; it can actually be the means by which his love is mirrored through your lives to the blessing of others as well.

# STUDY GUIDE

This chapter-by-chapter study guide has been produced to help you work through the book using the questions as a basis for discussion.

We recognize that the book may be used as background reading for a group, such as a marriage preparation class or home Bible study. The questions have been designed to encourage both group discussion and personal reflection.

The theme of each chapter is taken up with several questions designed to draw out individual comments. They are discussion-starters, so no answers are provided. Some of the questions are more appropriate for personal reply, rather than in the context of group work. These have been placed as the final question in each section.

## 1. Happily ever after?

1. Read Genesis 2:18–25. What do these verses teach us about God's idea of marriage?
2. Using the four words from the quotation of Charles Swindoll (see pp. 14–15) – severance, permanence, unity and intimacy – discuss what you think these words mean. Why are they important?
3. Take one or more of the real-life case studies that are described in this chapter. What would you have done in the same situation? How could the particular problems of each couple have been tackled earlier?
4. Read through the seven questions at the end of the chapter

(p. 27). Discuss with your partner your personal responses to each question. You may find it helpful to spend a few minutes praying together about your answers to these questions.

## 2. Building your marriage

1. Look at the two different views of marriage: 'Building' and 'Maintenance' (see p. 29). How do you view marriage?
2. Discuss the 'triangle principle'. Does this help you understand God's plan for marriage more clearly?
3. Go through the list of pressure points in marriage and some of the major causes that lie behind breakdown. Can you identify with any of these?
4. Spend some time considering the 'four pillars'. Evaluate your own relationships in each of these areas: physical, emotional, spiritual and social. Can you identify some strengths and weaknesses?

## 3. Two into one

1. Did your list of five adjustment areas correlate with the survey? How do you think you have coped with them? If you are engaged, how do you think you could prepare for those adjustments?
2. Refer back to the section entitled 'Side by side' and consider the five steps suggested to help in the adjustment process. Are there other steps you would add to this list? Taking one of the adjustments listed, discuss what could have been done to resolve the difficulty.
3. How do you relate to your wider family? Note some of the ways in which relationships with your relatives can be improved.
4. What has been the hardest adjustment that you personally, as a husband or wife, have faced? Spend some time talking

about this honestly together and conclude with a short time of prayer, focusing on those areas where you need to grow.

## 4. We don't talk any more

1. Read John and Anne's comments quoted at the start of the chapter. If they were your friends, what advice would you give to help them?
2. In the section 'Learning to communicate', there are seven suggestions to improve communication between husband and wife. Spend some time discussing each of these points and looking at ways in which they can build into your own relationship.
3. What are the main causes of disagreements between the two of you? How could you establish better communication to prevent them developing into major disagreements?
4. Ask your partner the following questions:
   Am I a good listener when you are sharing a concern?
   Do I express my feelings well in a way that you can understand and accept?
   Do I react differently from you when a conflict arises?
   Do I give you enough opportunity to talk about our relationship and, if not, how can I make more time?

## 5. Partners with God

1. Are you growing spiritually as individuals and as a couple? Discuss your answers and talk about your frustrations.
2. Discuss the five helps towards spiritual growth mentioned in the chapter: personal growth; prayer and the Word of God; belonging to a local church; giving; and serving.
   Are there areas of need in your own lives?
3. 'Serving God and serving others is the way to create a healthy outflow for your faith' (p. 107). Talk about some of the ways in which you can both become more effective in

serving God and others, bearing in mind the balance needed in your lives.

4. Discuss the ways in which you spend time with God. Do you need to establish a more regular pattern in your lives for praying and studying the Bible together? Take a few minutes to pray for each other. (For those with non-Christian partners, begin to look around for someone who will pray with you and for you regularly.)

## 6. Loving and learning

1. Think about this statement from the chapter (p. 115): 'But just as the world (or at least part of it) has overrated sex, we must quickly admit that at times ... the Christian church has been guilty of undervaluing it.' Do you agree with this? Can you think of any personal experiences to support your view?

2. Look again at the section entitled 'Family planning'. Spend a few minutes discussing the practical information in these sections, and consider some of the ethical issues which could be raised.

3. How important is it for a married couple to be open with each other about their past life? In what ways can a couple develop greater openness in their physical relationship?

4. If you are married, think about the illustration of the electric and gas ovens. Now talk over with your partner your sexual needs and responses and be prepared for your partner to do the same. For those preparing for marriage, talk about some of the things you have learned from reading this chapter.

## 7. Building a home

1. Think for a few moments about some of the homes you have visited as a couple. What are the qualities that are

particularly attractive to you in the place and the people who live there? List some of the specific things that you have seen and that you would like others to notice in your own home.

2. *For him:* How do you see your role as a partner in building a home? List your priorities as you understand them.
*For her:* What does it mean to be a homemaker?
Now swap your individual answers, and discuss them.

3. Look at the sections 'Money matters' and 'Planning your time'. Are there specific suggestions here that you can adopt to improve your management of finances and time? Talk these through together.

4. Make a list of some people you can invite to your home over the next few months. Go beyond your usual circle of friends and spend some time praying and thinking together about those who would benefit from a meal and friendship.

## 8. Starting a family

1. Refer back to the section 'Deciding to start a family'. Talk about your feelings as you consider the key questions.

2. Every newborn baby has certain basic needs. Make a list of those needs as you understand them. From your own experience of childhood, is there one thing you would like your children to experience and one thing you would like them to avoid?

3. As you face parenthood, what do you most look forward to and what do you most dread?

4. Consider the rules for raising delinquent children. Write some rules for raising children in a Christian family. (Remember to reassess when you have children of your own!)

# Epilogue: You don't bring me flowers

1. Spend a few minutes discussing each of the four words that are used to sum up commitment in marriage: affirmation, demonstration, evaluation and communication.
   In your own words, what does each of these mean? Which areas do you struggle with?
2. How do you work at keeping romance alive in your marriage?
3. Make two lists as described in the chapter. Begin by working on your own lists. Head them 'Things I thank God for in my marriage' and 'Things I need God to help me with in my marriage'. Compare your lists and discuss them together. Conclude with a short time of prayer in which you use the lists as a basis for talking to God.

# MOVING ON
## TOGETHER

We hope you have enjoyed reading *Friends, Helpers, Lovers.*
Here are some resources you may wish to make use of as you
move on together in marriage.

## Useful addresses

Family Planning Association
27–35 Mortimer Street
London W1N 7RJ
Tel. 0171-636 7866

Relate
Herbert Grey College
Little Church Street
Rugby
Warwicks. CV21 3BX
Tel. 01788 573241

National Childbirth Trust
Alexandra House
Oldham Terrace
London W3 6NH
Tel. 0181-992 8637

Care for the Family
136 Newport Road
Cardiff CF2 1DS
Tel. 01222 494431

Catholic Marriage Care
Clitheroe House
1 Blyth Mews
Blyth Road
London W14 0NN
Tel. 0171-371 1341

## Training courses

A number of Christian organizations run 'encouraging marriage'
programmes and courses. Some run residential weekends,
others concentrate on weekly classes.

   Care Trust provide a help line from their Glasgow office

(tel. 0141-332 7212), and they offer helpful advice on the types of programmes available across the UK. They will provide addresses and telephone numbers of relevant organizations on request.

## Books and videos

*The Adam and Eve Factor.* Four video programmes, dealing with the themes of commitment, conflict, intimacy and servanthood in marriage.

*Time For Each Other.* Video presentation with TV presenter Sally Magnusson looking at marriage from a Christian perspective, with sketches and real-life stories. (Workbook supplied with each tape.)

Both videos are available from Scripture Press, Ranns Road, Amersham-on-the-Hill, Bucks. HP6 6JQ (tel. 01494 722151).

*Marriage Matters.* A two-volume video of seminars by Rob Parsons. Issues included are communication, handling time pressures, resolving conflict, sex in marriage, expectations and realities. Available from Care for the Family.

There are several books dealing with sexual fulfilment in marriage, including *The Act of Marriage*, by Tim and Beverley La Haye (Marshall Pickering), *Intended For Pleasure*, by Ed and Gaye Wheat (Scripture Union) and *A Touch of Love,* by John and Janet Houghton (Kingsway).

Two books that helpfully deal with deeper and more honest relationships are *Loving Against the Odds*, by Rob Parsons (Hodder and Stoughton), and *Till the Heart be Touched*, by Gordon and Gail MacDonald (Highland Books).